MARCO POLO

Tips

UNITED ARAB EMIRATES

IRAQ · IRAN · AFGHA-NISTAN

UNITED ARAB EMIRATES · PAKI-STAN

SAUDI ARABIA · Tropic of Cancer

INDIA

SUDAN · OMAN · Arabian Sea

ERITREA · YEMEN

ETHIOPIA · INDIAN OCEAN

SOMALIA

915
.357
Wob
2013

www.marco-polo.com

SYMBOLS

INSIDER TIP	Insider Tip
★	Highlight
●●●●	Best of ...
⌁	Scenic view

☺ Responsible travel: fair trade principles and the environment respected

(*) Telephone numbers that are not toll-free

PRICE CATEGORIES HOTELS

Expensive	over 880Dh
Moderate	480–880Dh
Budget	under 480Dh

Prices for a double room with taxes, but without breakfast

PRICE CATEGORIES RESTAURANTS

Expensive	over 100Dh
Moderate	50–100Dh
Budget	under 50Dh

Prices for a typical dish, no drinks

On the cover: Al Arsah souk in Sharjah p. 68 | A history lesson at the Dubai Museum p. 53

CONTENTS

Ajman, Umm al-Qaiwain → p. 72

Ras al-Khaimah → p. 78

Fujairah & East Coast → p. 86

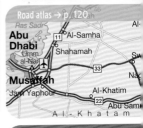
Road atlas → p. 120

DID YOU KNOW?

MAPS IN THE GUIDEBOOK
(122 A1) Page numbers and coordinates refer to the road atlas
(0) Site/address located off the map. Coordinates are also given for places that are not marked on the road atlas

INSIDE BACK COVER:
PULL-OUT MAP →

PULL-OUT MAP 🛇
(🛇 A–B 2–3) Refers to the removable pull-out map

The best MARCO POLO Insider Tips

Our top 15 Insider Tips

INSIDER TIP An excursion to Omani fjords

Take an adventurous boat trip in an Arab *dhow* in Musandam (photo below) → p. 93

INSIDER TIP An old seafarer

The *Museum of Ahmed Bin Majid* lies hidden in Ras al-Khaimah → p. 81

INSIDER TIP Bibliophile wonderland

Book World *Kinokinuya* is the name of this enormous bookshop in Dubai Mall. With half a million titles from every genre and area of interest, it is a sight to behold → p. 55

INSIDER TIP Aloo Gobi and Palak Paneer

The small Indian restaurants in the UAE serve food that tastes just as it does in Delhi. The favourite address of many of the locals is the *India Palace* in Abu Dhabi, where authentically prepared Indian dishes are served at very low prices → p. 39

INSIDER TIP Treasure trove for oriental fabrics and souvenirs

Coriander and cinnamon in jute sacks, brocade and printed cotton, cuddly camel toys for children and Bedouin-style cushions – shopping in the small shops of the historical *Souk al-Arsah* in Sharjah is much nicer than in the modern, air-conditioned shopping mall → p. 68

INSIDER TIP Mangroves in the Gulf of Oman

Go bird-watching by boat in the lagoon of *Khor Kalba*, the oldest mangrove swamp in Arabia → p. 99

INSIDER TIP Sky above the desert

Between Jebel Hafeet, a mountain rising out of the desert, and the sand dunes around Al Ain, which can reach a height of 100m (328ft), the landscape is ideal for a trip in a hot air balloon. You may even spot gazelles and camels on your flight → p. 41

BEST OF ...

FOR FREE

● *Colourful underwater world*

Schools of colourful Pacific Ocean fish and hovering rays are just some of the inhabitants of this dazzling underwater world. And looking through the huge glass window of *Dubai Aquarium* on the ground floor of Dubai Mall doesn't cost a single dirham (photo) → p. 55

● *Dizzying views*

You have to pay 400Dh for the privilege of enjoying the views from Burj Khalifa's viewing platform; you can get a similar view from *Bar Neos* on the 63rd floor of The Address hotel, and you only have to pay for your drink → p. 57

● *Magnificent mosque*

Non-Muslims have access to *Sheikh Zayed Grand Mosque* in Abu Dhabi, a mosque that is almost an architectural wonder of the world and is a breathtaking sight to behold. Every visitor is bowled over by its enormous dimensions and magnificence → p. 38

● *Dancing water fountains*

Between Arab-style palaces, dozens of water fountains shoot into the sky, in time with the classical music. Experience this Dubai spectacle after dark, when an accompanying light show can also be appreciated → p. 53

● *A different kind of city tour*

Free shopping buses to Dubai Mall and back depart from various parts of town – just wait at the stops, climb on the bus and start your improvised city tour → p. 57

● *Culture in the Qasr al-Hosn*

Arab gardens, art treasures, an extensive library, cultural events and much more can be experienced in Abu Dhabi's fort. *Qasr al-Hosn* is a cornerstone of the UAE's history and a meeting place for the population → p. 37

●●●●● Dots in guidebook refer to 'Best of ...' tips

● *Emirate cuisine*
In the *Al Dhafra-Restaurant* next to the Heritage Village of Abu Dhabi you can experience the diverse dishes of pan-Arab cuisine, as well as enjoy some specialities specific to the Emirates → p. 39

● *High-level shopping spree*
For four weeks it's all about shopping: during the annual *Dubai Shopping Festival* there are huge discounts, firework displays and an accompanying cultural programme → p. 108

● *Arabesques for hands and feet*
UAE women have appreciated the art of temporary tattooing with henna for centuries. Have yourself beautified in the same way in one of the many small henna studios found all over the Emirates, such as in the magnificent *Souk Madinat Jumeirah* in Dubai → p. 56

● *Shopping in a souk*
Basmati rice in huge sacks, cinnamon sticks, cardamom and exotic essential oils – the sights and smells in the alleys of Dubai's spice souk are a truly authentic experience. And haggling for the best price is all part of the fun → p. 55

● *Quads and camels*
The red and gold sand dunes known as 'Big Red' get particularly busy at the weekends. You can race through the dunes on a quad bike or go at a more leisurely pace on a camel → p. 59

● *Between palm trees and falaj irrigation systems*
A walk in the oasis of *Al Ain*, shaded by palm trees and surrounded by mud walls, will take you past lush plantations watered by ancient falaj irrigation systems, which bring water rising in the mountains to the fields (photo) → p. 46

● *A fort in Fujairah*
Step back in time in the old clay fort in Fujairah's dilapidated Old Town. Watchtowers, battlements and defensive structures as well as traditional meeting rooms have survived the many changes that have taken place elsewhere → p. 88

ONLY IN

BEST OF ...

● **Shopping XXL**

International fashion designers, top Arab designers, the world's finest jewellers and many exclusive brands are represented in the luxurious, gigantic and fully air-conditioned *Dubai Mall* – you will only break into a sweat when you are pulling out your credit card (photo) → p. 55

● **Downhill fun**

You have to dress up warm in Dubai's *indoor ski arena*: it snows all year round here and that's why the skiing and sledging are excellent. Beginners can even hire a ski instructor → p. 56

● **Marina Mall**

With its architecture and location, and superb views over Abu Dhabi's skyline, *Marina Mall* is one of the most popular shopping temples in the emirate. Begin a visit in one of the cafés on the top floor and be sure to visit the basement, where you can buy fabrics, shawls and jewellery at small stalls → p. 40

● **Among hammerheads and rays**

Watching marine creatures swimming about in their underwater worlds is amazingly relaxing. *Sharjah's* superbly designed aquariums and the surrounding area are a lovely place to spend time → p. 66

● **Amid gold and marble**

The extravagant interior of the *Emirates Palace* hotel in Abu Dhabi is worth seeing. Book a tour of the hotel, with time to view its exhibition about the museum island of Saadiyat, currently under construction, and to then enjoy afternoon tea from silver pots in the café → p. 37

● **Museum in a fort**

The *National Museum of Ras al-Khaimah*, one of only a few historic buildings in the Emirates that has received top-quality restoration, will take you back into a pre-oil past → p. 81

HEAT

RELAX AND CHILL OUT
Take it easy and spoil yourself

● *Afternoon tea opposite the fairytale mosque*
Take a seat on the terrace of the classy and attractive *Shangri-La* hotel in Abu Dhabi. When the silhouette of the domed and snowy white Sheikh Zayed Mosque is reflected in the lagoon before you, you will feel transported into the world of 'The Arabian Nights' → **p. 41**

● *Visit an Arabian hammam*
The magnificent *Royal Mirage* hotel is one of Dubai's best addresses. Its outstanding spa is open to non-residents. Pamper yourself with a massage in the Moroccan hammam → **p. 58**

● *Time out in a waterbus*
Exhausted from all the sightseeing in Dubai? How about a *Waterbus Tour*? Board it in the Heritage Village, put your feet up and enjoy the lively goings-on on the Creek. Twenty-five minutes later you can disembark, refreshed and relaxed → **p. 56**

● *In the tranquillity of the desert*
Set off to Liwa Oasis, just a two-hour drive from Abu Dhabi. This collection of villages is surrounded by white sand dunes. The luxurious yet rustic *Qasr al-Sarab* hotel is a great place to take a breather and enjoy the unique atmosphere of the desert (photo) → **p. 44**

● *Six Senses at Zighy Bay*
This spa, with its watercourses, fountains, limestone walls and steam bath, under a huge dome in the style of a traditional hammam, is a wonderful place in which to relax. Experienced staff offer a host of beauty and wellness treatments
→ **p. 93**

● *Big wheel above Sharjah*
After a stroll along the artificial canal of Qanat al-Qasba, sit back and relax in one of the air-conditioned glass capsules of the *Eye of the Emirates* for truly stunning views → **p. 66**

INTRODUCTION

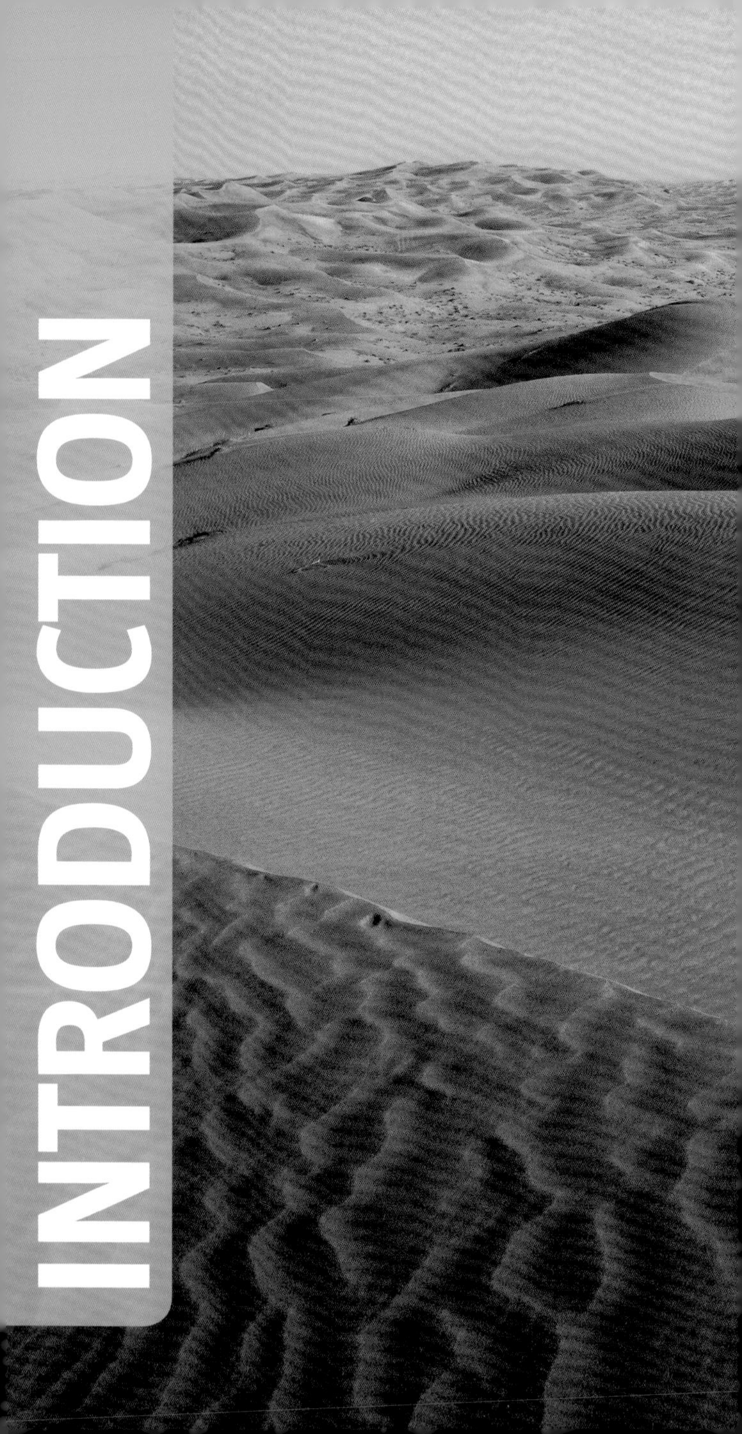

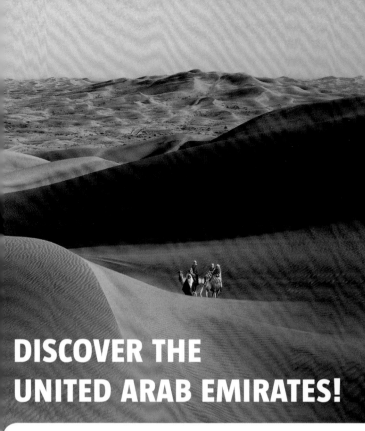

DISCOVER THE
UNITED ARAB EMIRATES!

Sand and sunshine are two commodities that the countries in the southeast of the Arabian Peninsula have always had in abundance, but in the 1960s they also discovered oil, the magic wand with which the people of the region reinvented their world. Where the ground was once covered by sand, today the sky is reflected in ponds and lakes, hills are covered by lawns, and ambitious architecture, even artificial islands, create a dramatic cityscape. Computers control the irrigation of countless tropical plants, and large palm trees line the urban highways, meticulously maintained by a legion of gardeners from Asia.

Alongside typical Arabian souks, bazaars full of traditional crafts and exotic scents, are many luxury shopping malls, which amaze visitors with their extravagant architecture and huge range of expensive goods. Holiday dreams of a sun-drenched paradise come true on the silky white sands of the hotel beaches. For a change, take a journey of discovery into the desert, where you'll spot wild camels and antelopes, to one of the beautifully restored old towns, or go to see Palm Jebel Ali, one of the 21st-century wonders of the world.

Photo: Desert dunes in Abu Dhabi

After the unification of the emirates in 1971 the seven rulers (emirs) agreed on a common foreign, defence and economic policy, but the individual emirates are still largely autonomous. Abu Dhabi and Dubai developed into hyper-modern cities, fuelled by the oil boom. Preparations are already being made for the time when the oil runs out, estimated to be in 20 to 40 years' time in Dubai and in around 100 years' time in Abu Dhabi. The economy is diversifying, with tourism an increasingly valued source of income for the whole of the UAE.

In light of the total area of the UAE being just 86,000 sq km, it does not take long to travel from one emirate to another. It is just 140km (88mi) from Abu Dhabi to Dubai, and the northernmost emirate, Ras al-Khaimah, is only another 90km away. They are linked by broad highways running through the desert. Dubai, a sheikhdom of just 3900sq km, keeps the world on the edge of its seat with its evermore audacious, record-breaking structures. Its famous artificial islands, where expensive hotels and holiday villas cater for the super-rich, are the most dramatic evidence of Dubai's appetite for innovation. It also has the second-largest shopping mall in the world, the highest building on earth, enormous artificial marinas, encircled by a skyline of skyscrapers; on almost every visit to Dubai you'll find something new, worthy of superlatives. Protecting the environment and the climate are not yet big issues here, as is demonstrated by Dubai's ice rinks, ski slope and countless air-conditioned malls. If a green project is undertaken, then it's for image reasons rather than out of environmental convictions.

Those with a taste for traditional Dubai are drawn to the Creek, the arm of the sea that flows through Dubai. As has been the way for decades, the passage to the other side is still in loud, open barges that smell of diesel, and peopled by migrant workers from India and Pakistan. On the Bur Dubai side, you can still discover a network of narrow streets between the imposing commercial establishments; heavily restored, smart and clean, the old quarter presents a picture-book image of Arabia.

570–632
Mohammed, Allah's prophet. The Islamic calendar begins with his flight from Mecca to Medina (622)

1507–1650
The coast of the Arabian Gulf is under Portuguese control

18th century
Bedouins settle on the coast of the Persian Gulf

19th century
The sheikhdoms in the south of the Gulf become known in Europe as the 'pirate coast'; in 1835 Great Britain signs protectorate treaties with the emirates, eliminating piracy and controlling foreign policy

Such colourful thirst-quenchers are piled high in the many markets of the emirates

The only places to see what Dubai was like before the oil boom are the museums, where yellowing black-and-white photographs depict dusty streets, wind-tower houses made of coral, and Sheikh Rashid bin Saeed al-Maktoum, drinking tea, riding a camel or engaging in falconry. Such scenes are very much pictures of the past. When oil was discovered in 1958, the world courted the Bedouin ruler, who used the oil billions to turn the small trading port into the fastest growing city in the world, where his subjects enjoyed a life of ease and luxury. Nonetheless, following the international financial crisis of 2008 real-estate prices fell here too, with many building sites put on hold at the end of 2011, including Palm Jebel Ali and The World.

1958
Oil is found in Abu Dhabi and then in Dubai

1970
Great Britain leaves the region on the Arabian Gulf

1971
The emirates Abu Dhabi, Dubai, Sharjah, Ajman, Umm al-Qaiwain, Fujairah and (1972) Ras al-Khaimah join forces to become the United Arab Emirates (UAE)

2004
The ruler of Abu Dhabi and first president of the UAE (since 1972), Sheikh Zayed Bin Sultan al-Nahyan, dies. He is succeeded in both of these offices by his son Sheikh Khalifa Bin Zayed

Abu Dhabi is also obsessed with being 'higher, more expensive, more spectacular'. The richest of the emirates, thanks to its vast oil reserves, it gave its citizens the imposing Sheikh Zayed Grand Mosque, an oriental dream of marble and gold that took ten years to build, and the Emirates Palace hotel, which is so magnificent as to have an air of an Arabian Versailles. Currently, a number of well-known architects are building not one, but several museums on the 'Island of Happiness'.

Sharjah, whose capital is just 15km (9mi) from Dubai, is the third-largest emirate and in recent years has made a name for itself as being an important cultural centre in the Arab world. The capital has superbly restored old palaces, excellent museums and galleries, and has been proclaimed the 2014 Islamic Capital of Culture. Since Sharjah has little oil, the emirate began focusing on tourism as early as the 1970s.

Future projects in the other four sheikhdoms are somewhat more modest: Ajman, Fujairah, Umm al-Qaiwain and Ras al-Khaimah do not have oil. Life here is far less glamorous than in Dubai and Abu Dhabi, and the past still lingers: many people still make a living in time-honoured ways, such as agriculture and fishing, and some of the towns still have a traditional Arab appearance. These emirates are dependent on the financial aid of Abu Dhabi, Dubai and the overall budget of the United Arab Emirates. Such support has allowed the development of good infrastructure, with several spectacular construction projects. Five-star hotels attract visitors who appreciate the lower prices and more relaxed atmosphere of the smaller emirates. Among their important tourist attractions are the sandy beaches of Ras al-Khaimah and Fujairah as well as the majestic Hajar Mountains.

What was true in the past is still true today: the ruling dynasties own the land and therefore also the oil. But the sheikhs allow their people to share in their wealth; young married couples are given homes, water, electricity and zero-interest loans, and education, training, pensions and care for the elderly are paid by the state. The per capita income and standard of living are among the highest in the world, which may be why the Arab Spring of early 2011 did not have repercussions in the UAE. Two neighbouring states, Yemen and Bahrain, experienced

Less glamorous: the emirates without oil

2006
The ruler of Dubai, Sheikh Maktoum, dies. He is succeeded by his brother Mohammed Bin Rashid al-Maktoum, which also makes him the vice-president and prime minister of the United Arab Emirates

2009
The global financial and economic crisis reaches the UAE

2010
The tallest building in the world, Burj Dubai is renamed Burj Khalifa, in recognition of Sheikh Khalifa Bin Zayed for providing support to Dubai during the world financial crisis.

Tradition and modernity coexist, and mosques between skyscrapers (here: Sharjah) are part of the cityscape

serious protests; in Bahrain, Saudi and Emirates troops were drafted in to support the king and the situation calmed down.

The region is easy to access for Europeans. After just a six- or seven-hour flight passengers arrive in a land of constant sunshine, long sandy beaches lapped by the warm waters of the Arabian Gulf and the Indian Ocean, desert adventures, and outstanding service and luxurious hotels. At first glance, Abu Dhabi and Dubai seem not much different from their Western models. This is a false impression, however, because the Arab way of life and traditions are nurtured even in these hyper-modern surroundings. Prayer, in the home or at the mosque, still structures the lives of the locals, and camel racing and falconry are the most popular hobbies – after shopping and luxury cars.

Shopping and luxury alongside falconry and camel races

The United Arab Emirates is not just for visitors who want to sit by a pool and go shopping: excellent roads make it easy to travel independently through remote desert landscape (just watch out for camels, which cross the roads from time to time). Organized tours will take you into a landscape of high sand dunes that shimmer red and yellow in the sunlight, or into the Hajar Mountains, which twinkle in the morning sun. It is magnificent scenery, unchanged for millennia, and hospitality, a cornerstone of Arab life, is guaranteed.

WHAT'S HOT

1 After Dark

Night-time golf Often the hot daytime sun is most suited to doing nothing. But after the sun sets, the locals get active. They play golf, for example. Thanks to floodlit courses at *Sharjah Golf and Shooting Club (Dhaid Road, 3rd Interchange, Sharjah)* and *Al Hamra Golf Club (Al Hamra Village, Ras Al-Khaimah)* golf can also be enjoyed at night. The best time to practise your technique is after sunset at the driving range at *Arabian Ranches Golf Club (Arabian Ranches, Emirates Road 311, Dubai, photo).*

Fashionable

2

On trend The region's fashion designers bring an Arabian twist to international trends. Rabia Zargarpur makes flowing robes that satisfy Muslimas and fashionistas alike *(www.rabiaz.com).* Her colleague Aisha bin Desmel banks on rich fabrics and bright colours *(Jumeirah Road, opposite Mercato shopping centre, Dubai, aisha-bindesmal.com).* Zareena Yousif integrates artistic embroidery into her designs *(Zabeel House, Zabeel Road, Karama, Dubai, www.zareena.co, Foto).*

Monumental

3

Architecture The age of the building boom is over, but the impressive buildings remain. Discover Dubai on an architectural tour. You will learn about awe-inspiring structures such as Burj Khalifa and about hidden gems *(www.abctoursdubai.com).* If you are interested in the buildings of Abu Dhabi, Walid Ismail of *Desert Adventures* knows the city like the back of his hand *(www.desertadventures. com).* The TDIC (Tourism Development & Investment Company) website provides information about construction projects that are planned, under construction or on hold in Abu Dhabi *(www.tdic.ae).*

Good Night

Nightlife In the Emirates the night is not just for sleeping. Affluent expatriates, in particular, are creating an ever more exciting scene. While Dubai already has a lot on offer, the other emirates are slowly following suit. The hottest meeting place in Dubai is the *Buddha Bar*, where there's a good chance of running into a celebrity or two *(Al-Sufouh Road, www.buddhabar.com)*. The most popular venue in Abu Dhabi is *SAX (Al Markaziyah Le Royal Meridien, photo)*. In Fujairah the best place for nightlife is the *Fez Bar* in the *Hilton*, which regularly hosts concerts *(Al Ghurfa)*.

Typically atypical?

Photography The region's creative individuals are moving away from kitsch motifs such as camels and sand dunes. Instead, they are inspired by the wider world and taking a new look at their Arab home. One of them is Lateefa bint Maktoum, an internationally successful photographer and artist who lives in Dubai. Her haunting photographs depict colourfully clothed people in wide-open landscapes *(www.lateefabintmaktoum.com)*. Lamya Gargash also captures her home with a camera. She documents traditional building styles and interior views of homes as well as modern architecture *(www.lamyagargash.com)*. Hind Mezaina's winning style is based on lo-tech optics. She photographs everything from waterfalls to sand dunes with her Lomo camera *(hindmezaina.com)*. The Third Line in Dubai *(Al Quoz 3, www.thethirdline.com)* is an outstanding gallery exhibiting photographic and fine art.

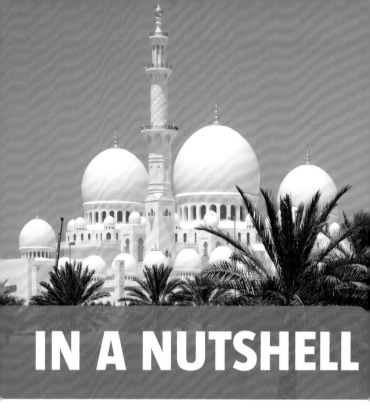

IN A NUTSHELL

CAMELS

On the Arabian peninsula, camels are the one-humped variety, or dromedaries. Dromedaries (also 'Arabian camel') are found in North Africa, southwest Asia (Arabian Peninsula) and more recently, Australia. Camels with two humps on the other hand live in Asia (Mongolia and India). Camels are status symbols, used for transport and carrying heavy loads; they provide milk and meat, and as racing camels they are beloved while also being investments. These Arabian camels were domesticated in this region 3000 years ago. They can cover 40km (25mi) a day and carry up to 300kg (650lbs) in the process. They can cope without food and water for several days. In the Emirates, camel racing is a popular spectator sport. In the winter season the racecourses are always very busy on weekends. Small robots are used to drive the camels.

DATES

A glass of tea and a handful of dates are still considered a traditional welcome for guests in the UAE. It is no surprise then that every hotel offers these healthy fruits to its guests at the breakfast buffet. The golden brown dates are two-thirds sugar, but also contain the most important vitamins and minerals and are full of fibre. They taste best when they are fresh, but are still very good a year later if dried. There are dozens of different types of dates in the UAE. The largest are stuffed with marzipan or almonds,

Falcons above the desert, *expatriates* and locals, irrigation systems and camel races – things worth knowing about the Arab world

wrapped in soft paper and packaged in wooden boxes or chocolate boxes, making them attractive souvenirs.

Date palms do not just grow around the oases in the UAE; they can also be seen growing in the cities. The 'trees of life' have always been appreciated for their many uses. As well as providing food and shade, the timber from the trunk can be used in construction or as firewood, and traditionally the leaves were used to make walls and roofs for barasti huts while the individual palm fronds were woven into baskets and mats, and their fibres wound into ropes. These palms begin bearing dates after eight years and are at their most fruitful after about two decades.

DESERT

The UAE is situated in the Earth's arid zone, on the edge of the Rub al-Khali desert. The desert has many different forms, as sand dunes, stony fields, and, by the sea, as a flat salt desert *(sabkha)*. Precipitation is rare and drains away very quickly. With a lot of effort and billions of dollars, attempts are being made to stop the desert from expanding further. With water from desalination plants parts of

Valuable 'pet': the falcon

the desert has become fertile, and parks, date-palm groves, gardens and agricultural areas have been established on formerly barren ground.

D HOW

The traditional Arab boat is still made by hand. The term dhow was introduced by Europeans for all Arab sailing boats, which all seemed the same to them. On the Arabian peninsula it refers to a traditional boat that has been used for fishing, pearl-diving and trading for centuries. Even though they're propelled by engines these days, rather than by their sails, their shape and appearance, material and manufacturing technique have remained the same. The timber, usually Indian hardwood (such as teak),

has to be imported. It is no longer held together by sisal, but by nails. There are different types of boats, of which sambuks, with an angular stern, are the most common; other types include the boom and the ghanjah. Arabs do not use the term dhow. They refer to them by their particular name for the type of vessel they are. Despite all progress and modernity, these old-fashioned boats are part of the Emirates' tradition, just like camels and falcons, and the nationals are very proud of them.

E CONOMY

The UAE contributes 3 percent to global oil production, but possess 10 percent of the world's oil reserves. In 2011 the Gross National Product was around 250 billion US dollars, of which around 30 percent came from oil and gas. The per capita income is 50,000 US dollars. Abu Dhabi's sovereign wealth funds hold more than 600 billion dollars, and its interest in Daimler AG is 9.1 percent – 'Abu Daimler' as the company says. The Emirates' foreign debt is 130 billion dollars, and Dubai is responsible for 80–100 billion dollars of this.

E NVIRONMENT

Even though the Emirates are primarily known for their spectacular construction projects, there have been some recent efforts to appear environmentally responsible. Instead of attracting further criticism for being wasteful with energy, as they have by operating ski slopes and ice rinks, Dubai and Abu Dhabi in particular are at pains to become leaders in climate protection, which is why they're investing billions in this area. Extensive parks are being set up and trees planted in all of the emirates. One outstanding project is the eco town of Masdar, designed by award-winning British architect Lord Foster. Still under construction, it is a completely carbon-neutral city in the desert, around 30km (19mi) east of Abu Dhabi. The university Masdar Institute of Science and Technology will focus on researching new green technologies. In order to show the inhabitants, both *nationals* and *expatriates*, the green way, there are annual environment days and repeat events such as *'plant a tree'*. Requests are also being made to be more conscious about air conditioning use, to save electricity and to pay attention to sustainable consumption.

FALAJ

The desert is alive on the Arabian Peninsula, where people have farmed the land for many centuries. The art of transporting precious water over long distances to irrigate palm groves and vegetable fields was vital. The oldest of these channels, carved into stone and made of extremely durable cement, known as *falaj*, are more than 2500 years old. This irrigation system is still in use in places in the UAE. It can be seen in Al Ain, Al-Dhaid, Wadi Hatta and Buraimi. In the Heritage Villages of Abu Dhabi and Dubai there are also replicas of ancient falaj systems.

FALCONS

The falcon is the heraldic emblem of the UAE. Young falcons are trained over several months by experienced falconers. Once the birds of prey have become used to humans and know their jobs, they are sold on. Out in the desert, the birds fly up from the outstretched arm and plummet down when they spot prey, after which they wait motionless for their master. The most valuable falcons are worth up to a million dirhams and their owners frequently take them to other Arab countries for hunting competitions. Foreign-

ers rarely see much sign of this century-old Arab passion, though falconry shows are put on by the Heritage Village of Abu Dhabi.

HORSES

Horses have been bred on the Arabian Peninsula for more than 2000 years and thoroughbred Arabian horses are still considered the most beautiful. Relatively small in size, they are intelligent, particularly fast and also have a lot of endurance. It is likely that their characteristics developed over thousands of years, since only a few foals managed to survive the unfavourable climatic conditions of the desert. The people of the Emirates love horses; they are highly esteemed by all classes of society. It is said that the prophet Mohammed had 100 horses with him during his flight from Mecca to Medina. Horse races are held every weekend during the winter months at the racecourses of the UAE, and the winners are awarded big prizes. The horse race with the biggest monetary prize in the world (6 million US dollars) is held in March in Dubai. The horses are kept in air-conditioned stables, and well looked after by caretakers and vets; they are fed special diets and also trained in horse pools.

ISLAM

Religion and everyday life are inseparable for devout Muslims. Belief in God governs all aspects of life. This God is transcendent, beyond human understanding. 'Bi ismi Allah, Ar-Rahmaani, Ar-Rahimi', 'In the name of Allah, the Beneficent, the Merciful', is a common saying; it is used on many different occasions to ask for divine blessings and seeks to integrate divine wisdom into everyday life. The Koran specifies exactly how Muslims are to behave in their daily lives. It is essential that they pray five times a day, with recitations and praise for Allah from the Koran, and they are also duty-bound to support the needy. What is also important is that Islam emphasises the unity of all the monotheistic religions. By this understanding Jesus is also a prophet and the gospels, like the Jewish Torah, are considered a revelation on a par with the Koran.

MOCKTAILS

For some time now every drinks list in every hotel bar and café has featured mocktails – non-alcoholic, often colourful, concoctions incorporating many kinds of fruit juices, that imitate their alcoholic counterparts. Currently very fashionable, they come in many different guises. How about a Virgin Colada or an Ipanema while watching the sunset? Every good bar has its own signature mocktail. A typical characteristic of UAE mocktails is that they contain date. You can also get proper cocktails incorporating alcohol, though not in Sharjah, which is alcohol-free.

POLITICS

Sheikh Khalifa Bin Zayed al-Nahyan, the Emir of Abu Dhabi, is the president of the federal state of the United Arab Emirates, which was founded in 1971. He is assisted by the Supreme Council, which consists of the emirs from the remaining emirates. However, the collaboration of the seven emirates is largely limited to foreign policy, economic policy, legal and defence matters. The prime minister is Dubai's ruler Sheikh Mohammed Bin Rashid al-Maktoum. The president and prime minister are elected by the Supreme Council for five-year terms; they can be re-elected any number of times. The remaining ministerial posts in the UAE are largely occupied by members of the ruling families. The government of the UAE and the sheikhdoms follow the feudal principle, meaning that there are neither parties nor unions. The emirs rule by decree. The local population are very satisfied with their government, not least on account of the many social benefits and the exceptionally high standard of living. Emiratis employed in public authorities, companies and hotels are paid a very generous minimum wage, which is much higher than the wages paid to *expatriates*.

POPULATION

Of the 8.2 million inhabitants of the UAE, only 948,000 are *locals* or *nationals*. Some 88 percent of the population (in Dubai 90 percent) are foreigners, migrant workers or *expatriates*, which is another world record for the country. The stellar economic rise from Bedouin settlements to global cities was only possible with the help of migrant workers, who made their know-how and their labour available. The majority are from India, Pakistan, Sri Lanka, the Philippines, Thailand, Bangladesh and other Arab countries. Since only migrant workers with a high income get a residency permit for their families, more than three-quarters of the population are male.

SHISHA

Strawberry, banana, and latte macchiato: the flavoured tobacco varieties offered in the shisha cafés in the UAE change depending on the season. When hookahs suddenly became popular among adolescent Europeans, the centuries-old former Bedouin passion changed in the Arab world too. More and more shisha cafés are opening in the cities and a growing number of women and tourists now appreciate the aromatic (albeit unhealthy) smoke and the relaxing bubbling of the water-cooled pipes (the reason hookahs are also known as *hubbly-bubbly pipes*). They have become an indispensable part of chilling out.

TRADITION & MODERNITY

Despite the hypermodern facade the past is still present in the UAE: in the camel market in Al Ain locals assess the animals before they start negotiating; women covering their faces stroll through the souks, their hands adorned with dark red henna patterns; people come together for the weekly camel races. But they also like to meet in the clubs of the luxury hotels, and you'll see Porsches, limousines and other luxury cars parked outside mosques, where their owners have gone to pray. Men dressed in white dishdashas meet their wives in the city's gourmet temples, holding the latest Blackberry in one hand and prayer beads in the other. Only family members and close friends are likely to have access to their homes, which are usually small palaces in the neo-Arabian style, with areas reserved solely for women, and others reserved for the men of the house.

WOMEN

The United Arab Emirates is among the most liberal countries of the Arabian Peninsula. Female Emiratis are in charge of their own assets, which is why they also play a significant economic role. They have their own schools and universities to prepare them for social and professional life, and women now outnumber men as students at the country's universities. There are four women ministers in the UAE; nine women among the 40 members of parliament (Federal National Council); and two-thirds of government employees and 40 percent of the people working in banks and the financial sector are women. In Abu Dhabi the first woman judge has been presented to the public.

Chilling out with a shisha is a centuries-old tradition

FOOD & DRINK

There is a delicious aroma in the air, a mix of cumin, coriander, fennel seeds, garlic and cinnamon, the highly fragrant spices that give the dishes of the Arabian Peninsula their special character. But it is not just Arab cuisine that gives the UAE a reputation for fine dining. The Emirates are a melting pot of nations, and cuisines from all over the world vie for popularity with diners, especially in Dubai and Abu Dhabi. Everyone here loves good, rich food, and enjoys eating out.

The choice of restaurants is particularly diverse in the four and five-star hotels. A large hotel can have up to a dozen different restaurants, including ones serving Indian, Japanese, French, Mexican, Italian and Lebanese cuisine.

The menus in Arab restaurants are dominated by lamb, chicken, rice and vegetables. Lamb and chicken (beef is uncommon and pork is taboo for religious reasons) are often marinated in yoghurt-based sauces, then grilled on charcoal. Rice is a popular accompaniment; basmati rice imported from India, a long-grain rice with a slightly nutty flavour and an unmistakable scent, is the preferred choice.

Lavish use of spices is typical. Cardamom, pepper, saffron and garlic are used in abundance. Crunchy flatbread is baked in charcoal ovens and served while it is still warm. Fish and shellfish, lobster and shrimp in particular, are also popular and come from the Arabian Gulf and the Indian Ocean; they are often simply

Photo: Burj Al Arab, Restaurant Al-Mahara

From award-winning restaurants to shawarma stalls – dishes for every taste and budget

grilled and served with garlic and limes. Typical starters in Arabia consist of little plates of pickled vegetables (cauliflower, carrots and peppers) and hummus, a chickpea puree made with sesame oil. Arab desserts are delicious confections, usually high in calories and incorporating plenty of honey and nuts, especially pistachios and almonds.

A traditional Arab breakfast includes flatbread, black olives, goat's cheese and yoghurt, served with black tea or coffee. Hotels put on large breakfast buffets that cater to every nationality: various types of bread and rolls, waffles and French toast, pastries (croissants, cakes etc.), fresh fruit and fruit salad, yoghurts, muesli, cornflakes, cold cuts, salmon, smoked fish, egg dishes, grilled tomatoes and fried sausages, fried potatoes, baked beans and sometimes also Japanese miso soup, Chinese dim sum (steamed dumplings stuffed with meat and vegetables) and sushi. This is accompanied by different kinds of juices, teas and coffees, including cappuccino.

LOCAL SPECIALITIES

▶ **achar** – vegetables pickled in vinegar and garlic: cauliflower, olives, carrots, onions, peppers

▶ **baba ghanoush** – aubergine puree with sesame oil

▶ **baharat** – spice mixture made of crushed pepper, coriander, cloves, cumin, nutmeg, cinnamon and paprika

▶ **baklava** – filo pastry dessert incorporating almonds, syrup and pistachios

▶ **chai** – black tea (usually sweetened)

▶ **ful medames** – cooked fava beans in a spiced tomato sauce, served with onions and vegetables

▶ **hummus** – chickpea puree with sesame oil (photo right)

▶ **khoubiz** – warm flatbread, used instead of a spoon when eating without cutlery (photo left)

▶ **labneh** – strained yoghurt, sometimes flavoured with garlic

▶ **ma madiniya** – mineral water

▶ **mashwee samak** – barbecued fish dishes

▶ **maskoul** – rice with onions

▶ **mahalabiya** – a creamy dessert with pistachios

▶ **muaddas** – rice with brown lentils

▶ **muhammar** – sweet rice with cardamom, raisins, rose water and almonds

▶ **mutabbal** – cooked aubergines with sesame paste and nut oil

▶ **qahva** – Arab coffee (usually served with cardamom, unsweetened)

▶ **shaurabat adas** – traditional Arab lentil soup

▶ **shawarma** – thinly sliced lamb or chicken from the spit with salad and yoghurt sauce, served in a flatbread

▶ **shish kabab** – grilled lamb, skewered

▶ **shish tawook** – marinated, grilled chicken, skewered

▶ **tabouleh** – salad of chopped parsley, diced tomatoes, cucumber, onion, bulgur and mint

▶ **wara enab** – vine leaves stuffed with flavoured rice

Sometimes it is even possible to get high-protein camel milk, which is low in calories.

Often, the hotels offer lavish buffets for lunch and dinner too. Typically, they change the culinary or geographic focus several times each week, with, say, Italian one day, Mexican the next, and then seafood or Indian.

On Friday, most hotel restaurants offer

brunch from late morning. This is one of the best ways of appreciating the country's multicultural nature, and the ways in which it shapes the culinary scene. The tables creak under the weight of all the tasty treats available: Italian antipasti, French hors d'œuvres, Arab vegetable specialities, Japanese sushi and Chinese dim sum are just some of the choices available.

The wide choice of eating options in the UAE ranges from simple snack bars and the food courts found in shopping malls to luxurious gourmet temples. In addition to other Arab and Asian cuisines, you will find African and Western restaurants, invariably run by *expatriates*, the 'guest workers' of the Arabian Peninsula. The choice is particularly good in Abu Dhabi and Dubai, where you can eat excellent (and also very inexpensive) Indian and Pakistani food.

The most expensive and elaborately designed restaurants are located in the luxury hotels. For cheap eating, seek out the food courts in the shopping malls, where self-service restaurants of every type, from fast food to Asian and Latin American places, fish restaurants and vegetarian outlets, exist side by side, sharing a central seating area. Alternatively, a delicious standby is *Shawarma* (warm flatbread filled with barbecued lamb or chicken and salad), which is sold both in the food courts and from street stalls.

Islam does not permit Muslims to consume intoxicating beverages. For that reason alcohol is sold only in hotels, licensed bars and clubs in the UAE. Sharjah is the only emirate where there is a strict ban on alcohol. Excellent and refreshing alternatives to alcohol include freshly squeezed juices, such as mango, papaya, banana and orange, which are served chilled everywhere. The 'mock-tails', imaginative combinations of different fruit juices, are quite wonderful.

An old tradition: an Arabian snack

Of course, local mineral water, such as Masafi, is sold everywhere, in large plastic bottles; the tap water here is safe, but it marred by a slight taste of sulphur on account of it being desalinated sea water.

SHOPPING

The people in the United Arab Emirates are proud of their trading traditions. Spices, gold and silver, brocades from India and silk from China: the people on the Arabian Gulf have always traded in luxury goods. For centuries they traded in souks, each one dedicated to a particular type of merchandise, with many small stalls next to each other – rugs in one street, saffron, cinnamon and cardamom in the next, cooking utensils in another. It was said that it was down to the will of Allah who the buyer found, and the competition stimulated business. With increasing wealth, the souks began to change. Today, most shops are housed in modern shopping complexes, which is less picturesque for visitors, but still typical. As well as traditional goods, you'll find electric goods and suitcases, plastic toys and kitchenware and cheap Western clothing. Anyone who enjoys shopping can spend days wandering through the malls, which are architecturally impressive and much more elaborately designed than their Western counterparts. The sheer size of the air-conditioned shopping arcades is impressive, and the vast expanses of glass, chrome and marble are alleviated by synthetic palm trees and gushing waterfalls. The latest international fashion collec-

tions can be found here, as well as speciality goods from all over the world, from English china to Swiss watches, lingerie from the United States and jigsaws from Germany. Nowhere else in the world is the selection greater or the prices so reasonable (thanks to the absence of taxes and customs duties). And if you begin to flag, you can revive in a huge choice of self-service cafés and fast food outlets. The ultimate shopping stronghold is Dubai, which has around 50 luxurious shopping malls, including the largest in the world – Dubai Mall, Mall of the Emirates.

ART

Sharjah's Arts Area in the old town is home to galleries selling paintings and objects by local artists. It's well worth visiting if you are interested in such things. The work presented ranges from modern, abstract art to objects that draw on Arab traditions.

DUBAI SHOPPING FESTIVAL

During the Dubai Shopping Festival all shops offer discounts of 20–40 percent and prizes worth millions of dirhams are given away every day. The event, which is as much about entertainment as shop-

Oriental souks and exciting shopping malls – shopping is a real experience in the United Arab Emirates

ping, also includes fashion shows, concerts and firework displays. When does this city go shopping crazy? From mid-January to mid-February. If you want to be part of this event, you must book your hotel early *(www.mydsf.com)*.

FASHION

The shopping malls are home to a large number of international designers (Armani, Chanel) as well as to young, modern labels such as Zara and Gap. Children's boutiques are also very common. Maps at the entrance list all the shops represented in the mall. Keep an eye out for special offers; you can get discounts of up to 50 percent when old collections are sold off in the end-of-season sales in September and February / March.

GOLD

The Gold Souk of Dubai is the most famous place for purchasing gold jewellery in the Emirates. You will not find another place where gold is cheaper or the choice of jewellery better. The price is determined by the weight of the item of jewellery you wish to purchase and that day's gold price: the decorative work, which is often very ornate, is done for free. In Abu Dhabi, the new Gold Souk is next to the Madinat Zayed Shopping Complex.

HOMEWARE

Goods from India and Indonesia are inexpensive. You can get small items that have been made to look old, such as picture frames, vases and sculptures. You can also get lovely (but expensive) rugs, pottery and wooden chests from Yemen. The biggest selection of such items can be found in the Central Souk (Blue Souk) in Sharjah, but almost every mall will have shops of this nature.

THE PERFECT ROUTE

INCREDIBLE WEALTH

① *Abu Dhabi* → p. 32 is the starting point for this trip through the Emirates. The first site of interest, which will have you reaching for your camera, is the spectacular *Sheikh Zayed Mosque* → p. 38. Afterwards walk along the Corniche, with views of the city's skyline, to the *Heritage Village* → p. 37. Enjoy afternoon tea in the *Emirates Palace Hotel* → p. 37. Finally, go to the fantastic *Shangri-La-Hotel* → S. 42 for your evening meal.

ANCIENT OASIS AT THE FOOT OF THE HAJAR MOUNTAINS

The highway makes its way through a flat sandy desert to the oasis of ② *Al Ain* → p. 44 (photo left). More than 200 springs feed the parks and green spaces. A stroll through the date palm groves of the oasis is romantic, while a visit to the exhibitions in *Al-Jahili Fort* → p. 46 will flesh out the history of Abu Dhabi. Continue to ③ *Hatta* → p. 59. The traditional summer resort of the citizens of Dubai, Hatta is full of palm groves, set against the rugged backdrop of the Hajar Mountains. Book a room in Hatta Fort Hotel and take excursions to the Heritage Village and the Hatta Pools (photo above).

HIGHLIGHTS IN DUBAI

Take a water taxi across the Creek in ④ *Dubai* → p. 50 and enjoy the incomparable atmosphere of one of the cafés on the Bur Dubai side, taking the time to plan your further sightseeing to *Burj Khalifa* → p. 53, the tallest building in the world (photo right) in Downtown Dubai, a quarter where old Dubai can still be found. Next, take the monorail to *The Palm Jumeirah* → p. 54. A visit to *Dubai Mall* → p. 55, containing the enormous Dubai Aquarium, and a stroll through the city's *souks* → p. 55 are also a must.

WIND TOWERS AND PALACES

10km (6mi) to the north is the emirate of ⑤ *Sharjah* → S. 60. Cafés and restaurants line the central area of Qanat al-Qasba, where locals and Asian guest workers meet. Enjoy a sweet chai in *Souk al-Arsah* → p. 68 after taking in the palaces and museums

Experience the rich variety of the United Arab Emirates on this tour from Abu Dhabi to Fujairah, with an excursion to Hatta

in the old town. ⑥ *Sharjah Desert Park* → p. 71, in the east of the city, is also worth a visit if you want to find out more about the wildlife of the desert.

CULTURE SHOCK

Dense traffic and lots of low concrete buildings characterise the northern emirate ⑦ *Ajman* → p. 73. But a walk around its streets will reveal its particular low-key atmosphere and pleasures. For just a few cents you can enjoy a drink in a teahouse, and you can eat outstanding and inexpensive food in one of the Indian restaurants. Next continue your journey (25km / 15mi) northwards to ⑧ *Umm al-Qaiwain* → p. 75. The main attraction here is the *Umm al-Qaiwain Museum* → p. 76, housed in the old fort, one of the few surviving buildings from the pre-oil era.

OLD ARABIA

Approximately 70km (43mi) further is ⑨ *Ras al-Khaimah* → p. 78. Its accommodation includes several good beach hotels and the splendid Khatt Springs Hotel, which is reminiscent of one of the

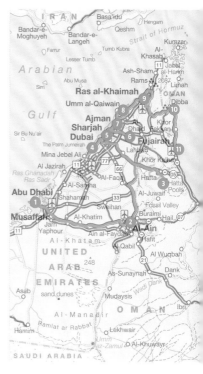

old Arab palace forts. Spend the following day visiting the old town as well as the well-run *National Museum* → p. 81. The drive through the Hajar Mountains to the east coast is attractive and will take you to ⑩ *Dibba* → p. 91, where you'll find pleasant and inexpensive beach hotels, suitable for a multi-day stay. On your way to ⑪ *Fujairah (city)* → p. 88 (20km / 12mi) you'll travel through beautiful scenery: rugged mountains shimmering in a bluish-grey haze, and palm groves, a lovely saturated green.

Around 650km (400mi).
Actual driving time: 8 hours.
Recommended time: 10–14 days
Detailed map of the route in the road atlas, the pull-out map and on the back cover

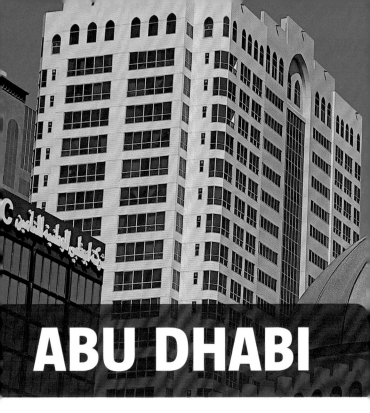

ABU DHABI

This ultra-modern capital, filled with skyscrapers and urban highways, also has uninhabited desert, mountain oases and undeveloped islands, but it has only recently begun investing in tourism.

Abu Dhabi, 160km (100mi) south of Dubai, is shaped by two opposites: the city and its surrounding area, where half of the emirate's 2.4 million inhabitants live, the locals in magnificent palaces and mansions and the guest workers, who make up 80 percent of the population, in modern skyscrapers; and the uninhabited desert, a landscape of shimmering sand dunes and dead-straight oil pipelines, which begins just outside the capital. So far, the coast here has few beach hotels, but there are 200 smaller

islands and islets off the coast, on which construction projects are gradually being realised. At the foot of Jebel Hafeet is the oasis of Al Ain, the seat of a university and several museums. Tourism is still small beer for Abu Dhabi, for the largest of the emirates, taking up four-fifths of the total area, possesses 95 percent of the UAE's oil reserves and 90 percent of its gas reserves.

Wealthy Abu Dhabi has virtually no old buildings, for all the old coral stone and clay buildings were pulled down during the city's construction and extension following the oil boom.

Only the historic emir's palace remains, charting Abu Dhabi's proud history. In 1761 the Nahyan family led the Bedouin tribe of the Bani Yas from the Liwa Oases

Photo: Khalifa Mosque in Abu Dhabi city

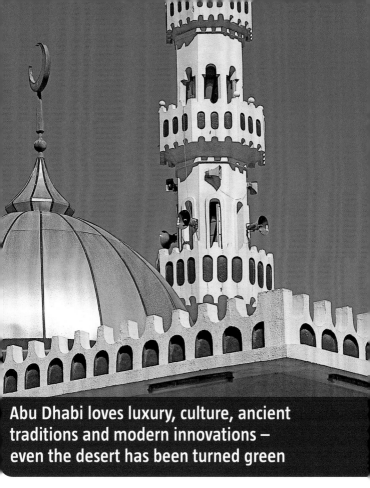

Abu Dhabi loves luxury, culture, ancient traditions and modern innovations – even the desert has been turned green

to a flat sandy island off the coast, where they had discovered a gazelle at a water hole. They built a settlement, Abu Dhabi ('father of the gazelle'), which became the seat of the sheikh and the emirate's capital in 1793. But even in 1960 Abu Dhabi was just a fishing village, whose inhabitants lived in small huts around the emir's fort. In just a few decades Abu Dhabi achieved unparalleled development to become the richest and most powerful of the Emirates.

ABU DHABI (CITY)

MAP INSIDE BACK COVER
(126 B1) (*m* G6)

The city of Abu Dhabi occupies an island, connected to the mainland by three bridges. Its attractions include a mosque, beautiful and colossal like no other, a hotel palace straight from 'The Arabian Nights', futuristic skyscrapers,

residential palaces in tropical parks and several beach hotels.

The start of the city's development as a tourist destination on the Arabian Gulf was the opening of the 1.6-billion-pound Emirates Palace hotel in 2005. In the previous years, construction focused mainly on creating infrastructure for the population and the increasing number of were wary of the emirate becoming as easy-going as Dubai, but did not want to go as far as introducing prohibition, as they had in Sharjah.

A green and modern metropolis is the first impression that visitors will receive of this desert city. Rebuilt completely after the oil boom, the city (now with approx. 1 million inhabitants) is charac-

The racetrack on Yas Island goes right through Yas Marina Hotel

expatriates. Unlike in Dubai, those with power in the emirate were against international tourism and did not promote tourism from Western countries. They

🏛 WHERE TO START?

Coaches stop at the main bus station opposite **Abu Dhabi Mall**. They make their way along Al Ferdous Street (10th Street) to Corniche East Park. With views of the city's skyline, it takes around an hour to get to Heritage Village (5km / 3mi). From there take a taxi to Sheikh Zayed Grand Mosque or to Yas Island.

terized not just by its impressive skyline, a forest of ultra-modern skyscrapers, but also by more than 20 parks and gardens. Lavish green spaces also flank the roads. At the northern end of Abu Dhabi is the 6 km (4 mi) Corniche Park. Starting at Maqta Bridge, Qurm Corniche, lined by date palms on its eastern side, leads into the centre; a mangrove swamp on the ocean side runs on for several kilometres. Abu Dhabi city is in a perpetual state of flux. New shopping malls are constantly springing up and enormous construction projects are always underway. The latest under is the world's first zero-emission city, designed by the renowned British architect Lord Foster. Called *Masdar* (spring or source) and located near the airport, on the outskirts of Abu Dhabi, it is intended for 50,000 inhabitants; it will be car-free and powered by wind and solar energy *(www.masdaruae.com)*. Opposite Abu Dhabi, on the island of Yas *(www.yasisland.ae),* which already has a Formula 1 racing track, a golf course, a marina and a Ferrari theme park (Ferrari World), there are plans to built Yas Mall and other leisure projects in the near future. Following the example of Dubai, Abu Dhabi is now also planning an urban railway. A grid network of 131km (81mi) is the goal.

A double-decker bus, run by Big Bus Tours, links the city's attractions, starting at Marina Mall and stopping in 11 places (including Sheikh Zayed Mosque, Emir- ates Palace, Heritage Village, Iranian Market). You can get on and off at will, and tickets are valid for 24 hours. *Daily 9am–5pm | departs every 30 mins, duration 2.5 hours | 200Dh, children 100Dh, families 500Dh | www.bigbustours.com*

SIGHTSEEING

BATEEN DHOW YARD
A craft that has now become rare in the Emirates is alive and well here. On a small island off the city's northern west coast (access via a causeway) is a boatyard where Indian and Pakistani carpenters manufacture traditional dhows by hand. *Bateen Street, from Bainunah Street (34th Street)*

⭐ Corniche Park
Palm trees and palaces on the water: stroll along Abu Dhabi's most impressive thoroughfare during the evening hours → p. 36

⭐ Emirates Palace
This Arabian dream palace is open to everyone wishing to enjoy a cup of tea or coffee → p. 37

⭐ Hili Archaeological Park
A Friday afternoon with the locals in Al Ain's archaeological park → p. 46

⭐ Sheikh Zayed Grand Mosque
A guided tour through the Emirates' largest and most beautiful mosque → p. 38

⭐ Camel Market
The last large camel market of the Emirates, on the outskirts of Al Ain → p. 46

⭐ Sir Bani Yas
Noah's Ark on an island: gazelles, antelopes and giant tortoises in the Wildlife Reserve → p. 44

⭐ Heritage Village
Camels, ancient irrigation systems and traditional handicrafts: the Heritage Village gives an insight into what life was like before the oil boom → p. 37

⭐ Al-Ain National Museum
Desert discoveries: archaeological evidence of 5000-year-old settlements → p. 45

⭐ Yas Island
Abu Dhabi's latest attraction does not just have a Formula 1 track and the theme park Ferrari World, it also has a real rarity in the UAE: cycle paths → p. 39

CORNICHE PARK ⭐

The 6km (4mi) promenade, which runs between the Sheraton hotel in the northeast and the Hilton in the west, has been turned into an elaborate park, with pedestrian walkways, bicycle paths, tropical flowers and date palms, as well as monuments, fountains and other water features. There are several view-

are also regular folklore events, concerts and film screenings. Take a break in the INSIDER TIP pretty gardens or in Delma Café on the first floor. *Closed for renovation until autumn 2012. Sat–Thu 8am–2pm and 5pm–8pm, Fri 5pm–8pm | entry 3Dh | Zayed the First (Electra) Street, corner of Rashid al-Maktoum Road (Airport Road), next to the Old Fort | www.adach.ae*

Nimble-fingered Indian guestworkers get fish out of the nets in Dhow Harbour

points, cafés, restaurants and picnic sites where you can take a break. Early in the mornings the park is popular with joggers, while after sunset it is filled with families out for an evening stroll. *Abu Dhabi Corniche*

CULTURAL FOUNDATION

Architecturally, the Cultural Foundation, built in 1980, is like a mix between a fort and a white palace: arcades with a hint of watchtower, surrounded by gardens. Exhibitions display ancient copies of the Koran, jewellery, handicrafts, archaeological finds and model dhows. There

INSIDER TIP DHOW HARBOUR

This is a good place to experience traditional Arabia. Fishing boats and the Al Dhafra restaurant ship are moored here, and you can haggle for rugs, pottery and textiles at the Iranian Souk, a treasure trove for typical souvenirs; anyone interested in carpets should go, as the name suggests, to the Afghan Carpet Souk. Al Mina Street *(3rd Street)* is home to the fish market *(daily 7am–10am and 4pm–7pm | at the end of Dhow Harbour)* as well as a fruit and vegetable market *(daily 7am–1pm and 4pm–7pm | between Al-Mina Street and Dhow Harbour)*.

EMIRATES PALACE ★ ●

This oriental fairytale palace is located on a hill and is surrounded by spectacular water features and 100ha (250 acres) of parkland. The 800-m (2600ft) long building is crowned by 114 domes adorned with gold leaf, illuminated by 1000 chandeliers made of Swarovski crystals, shaded by 8000 imported palm trees, and framed by a 1.3km (0.8mi) beach. The palace, which opened in 2005, serves as a luxury hotel, a conference centre and a government guesthouse. Spacious halls and corridors are extravagantly decorated with marble, granite, columns, stucco, chandeliers and gilded ceilings. Twenty restaurants, cafés and bars as well as two large pool complexes complete the ensemble. *Entry into the Saadiyat exhibition (see p.38) free, tour (with tea and cake) 100Dh, advance booking required | Corniche Road West | www.emiratespalace.com*

FALCON HOSPITAL

Some 4000 patients are treated every year in Abu Dhabi's falcon hospital by vet Dr Margit Müller and her team. Visitors can get an insight into the work of the clinic during a tour, which includes entry to its falconry museum. *Sun–Thu 10am and 2pm | 170Dh (children 60Dh) | Sweihan Road km 3 (near the airport) | tel. 02 5 75 51 55 | www.falconhospital.com*

HERITAGE VILLAGE ★

Situated right on the water and conceived as a kind of open-air museum, the Heritage Village is a complex of traditional workshops where handicrafts, including silver knives, leather goods and copper items, are manufactured. A well demonstrates how water was supplied and distributed in a typical village: an ox draws the water to the surface using an ancient contraption and a leather sack, and the water is subsequently channelled into several canals (falaj). A reconstruction of a souk, with a few palm-leaf huts (barasti), sells spices and ceramic goods, and there is a traditional teahouse where you can buy refreshments. Children can watch the goats, donkeys and falcons or muster the courage for a camel ride. A replica fort houses the Heritage Village Museum, with historic black-and-white photographs documenting Abu Dhabi's history, as well as Bedouin costume, jewellery, weapons, household items and an exhibition about pearl diving. The best time to visit the Heritage Village is in the evening when the locals also come here and the place is filled with activity. *Sat–Thu 9am–2pm and 5pm–9pm, Fri 2pm–8pm | entry 3Dh | Breakwater (at Corniche)*

QASR AL-HOSN ●

Surrounded by gleaming skyscrapers, the ancient fort of Qasr al-Hosn, built in 1793, embodies the history of Abu Dhabi like no other building in the emirate. For more than two centuries the fortified palace was home to generations of the Al-Nahyan ruling family. The building, which was called 'White Fort' by the British and 'Old Fort' by the locals, is the oldest in the emirates. Like the neighbouring Cultural

LOW BUDGET

▶ The Japanese shop Daiso in Eastern Road, Abu Dhabi *(1st floor in the Gold Centre, next to Madinat Zayed Shopping Centre)* and in Al-Ain in *Sheikh Khalifa Street (opposite Al-Noor Hospital)* you can buy food, stationery, cosmetics and all sorts of other things for less than back home.

Foundation, it is closed to visitors until the end of 2012 because of renovation works. *Sun–Thu 8am–1.30pm | free entry | Al-Nasr Street | www.adach.ae*

SAADIYAT

The emirate's most ambitious project, a spectacular 'cultural city', is currently

from a INSIDER TIP permanent exhibition, with models, in the *Emirates Palace hotel. Daily 10am–10pm | free entry | www.saadiyat.ae*

SHEIKH ZAYED GRAND MOSQUE ★ ●

This impressive building is fascinating, even from afar: four minarets and three

Sheikh Zayed Grand Mosque is open to non-Muslims

under construction on Saadiyat, the 'island of happiness', an island measuring 27sq km (10sq mi) 500m (540yds) off the coast of the city. It includes a Guggenheim Museum planned by Frank Gehry, a Maritime Museum designed by Tadao Ando, as well as a 60-m (200 ft) Performing Arts Centre by Zaha Hadid. Furthermore, Jean Nouvel has designed a cuboid outpost of the Paris Louvre and the British architect Lord Foster will build a Sheikh Zayed National Museum. It is intended that the project will be completed by 2018. Even though the island is still a construction site, you can already get an impression of what it will be like

large as well as 79 smaller domes create a striking image of the orient. The country's largest mosque, it is dedicated to the first president, Sheikh Zayed, who died in 2004. A forest of 1092 white columns, adorned with flowers and ornamental intarsia, delineate the rooms and courtyards. Before entering the prayer hall women are given concealing black abayas and scarves. Inside, there is a handmade carpet from Iran that covers more than 5000sq m (6000sq yds) and a multicoloured 15m (50ft) chandelier with 2 million Swarovski crystals, which was made in Germany. *Sat–Thu 9am–11.30am, free guided tours in Eng-*

lish Sat–Thu 10am, booking required | tel. 02 418 13 52, zayedmosquetour@adta. ae | free entry | Rashid al-Maktoum Road (Airport Road) South

YAS ISLAND ⭐

Yas Island, equipped with a golf course, a marina and many exciting buildings, is the latest attraction in Abu Dhabi. Further leisure facilities, including Yas Mall, with 500 shops, will be built here by 2015.

The world's largest indoor theme park, Ferrari World, has a rollercoaster that goes at 140kph (87mph) (Formula Rossa), a lift (G-Force) that catapults visitors 62m (203ft) into the air (higher than the roof), at 42kph (26mph), as well as many other attractions relating to Ferraris and car racing. *Sun, Tue, Wed noon–10pm, Thu–Sat noon–midnight | entry 225Dh (for those taller than 1.5m /4ft 11 ins), 165Dh (for those under 1.5m) | Yas Island | E10 exit Yas West | www. ferrariworldabudhabi.com*

Like Bahrain, Abu Dhabi is also attracting car-racing fans with a new Formula 1 racetrack. German circuit designer Hermann Tilke built the 5.53km (3.4mi) Yas Marina Circuit *(www.yasmarinacircuit. ae)* on Yas Island (east of the city of Abu Dhabi). It runs between the two buildings of the Yas Marina hotel and under its connecting bridge. It opened in November 2009.

☺ You can also INSIDER TIP explore Yas Island by bike. New cycle routes will take you across and around the island, past the Formula 1 racetrack and Ferrari World. *Mon–Sat 8.30am–5.30pm | 200Dh | Noukhada Adventures | Meena Street | tel. 02 6 50 36 00 | www.nouk hada.ae*

AL-DHAFRA ●

Next to the Heritage Village and with views of the capital's skyline, this restaurant serves Arab cuisine, including typical Emirates' dishes. *Breakwater | tel. 02 6 73 22 99 | Moderate*

AL-FANAR ♨

Get great views in the revolving restaurant at a height of 120m (390ft). This place serves international cuisine, including inexpensive lunches; the Friday brunch is popular. *Daily | Royal-Meridien-Hotel, 28th Floor | Sheikh Khalifa Bin Zayed Street | tel. 02 6 74 20 20 | www. lemeridien.com | Expensive*

CAFÉ FIRENZE

Serving pizza and pasta as well as Turkish coffee, this is a popular modern café in the Western style; the INSIDER TIP terrace is particularly 'in'. *Daily | Tariq Bin Zayed Street (centre) | tel. 02 6 33 10 80 | www.caféfirenzeuae.com| Budget*

INSIDER TIP INDIA PALACE

The decor here imitates a Maharaja's palace, and the extensive menu of Indian dishes completes the ambience in every way. Does not have an alcohol licence. *Daily | Al-Salam Street | tel. 02 6 44 87 77 | Moderate*

MARINA CAFÉ

This large circular building is located by the Breakwater and has good views of the Corniche skyline and the speedboats in the harbour. Serves international cuisine with meat and fish dishes, as well as burgers and salads; also offers shisha service. *18th Street (access promenade to the Breakwater) | tel. 02 6 81 64 40 | Moderate*

SHOPPING

ABU DHABI MALL
Smart and modern, this mall has several courts over four storeys, with some 200 boutiques selling clothes, shoes, jewellery and cosmetics, as well as a food court, self-service cafés and a huge supermarket. *Sat–Wed 10am–10pm, Thu 10am–11pm, Fri 3.30pm–11pm | 10th Street, next to the Beach Rotana Hotel | www.abudhabi-mall.com*

MADINAT ZAYED SHOPPING MALL
Has 400 shops in the moderate price range as well as several department stores, and also attracts visitors with its own gold souk. *Sat–Thu 10am–10pm, Fri 2pm–10pm | Eastern (Al-Sharqi) Street (4th St.)*

MARINA MALL ●
This is Abu Dhabi's most attractive mall. Under the white tent roof are four light-filled floors filled with shops of internationally famous brands, 20 restaurants and cafés, some of which have balconies and views of Abu Dhabi's skyline. The basement has a supermarket and inexpensive stalls selling scarves and jewellery. Other attractions include a massive entertainment complex with a bowling alley, an ice rink as well as an indoor ski slope (currently under construction). The mall's west side has a good view of the Emirates Palace hotel. *Daily 10am–10pm | Breakwater, from Corniche Road West | www.marinamall.ae*

BEACH

CORNICHE BEACH
The artificial public beach between the Hilton and Arabian Gulf Street is useful for visitors who are staying in a hotel without beach access. It possesses changing rooms, toilets, a garden, parasols, cafés and a coast guard. *Daily 7am–11pm | entry 5Dh | Corniche Road West, opposite the Heritage Village*

Marina Mall, Abu Dhabi's most attractive mall, has entertainment as well as shopping

SPORTS & ACTIVITIES

INSIDER TIP KHALIFA PARK

This large park in the south of the city has a miniature train, canal with abras, fountains, ponds, water displays, a maritime museum, an aquarium and an open-air theatre (falconry demonstrations) with 3200 seats. *Daily 8am–10pm | entry 5Dh | Eastern Ring Road (8th Road), behind Al-Bateen City Airport | Al-Matar*

LULU ISLAND ☼

Lulu Island is an artificial island off Abu Dhabi's north coast, between Breakwater and Mina Zayed. Around 6sq km (2sq mi) in size, it has two lakes, beaches, cafés and restaurants, situated between artificial sand dunes and reached by an open miniature train.

The island is a great place to get a comprehensive view of Abu Dhabi's skyline. Shipping in the vicinity has temporarily stopped because of expansions to the leisure island.

ORIENTAL SPA & FITNESS

This women-only fitness centre offers gym and fitness suites, aerobics classes, a pool and various massage and spa treatments. *Sat–Thu 9am–10pm, Fri 3pm–10pm | Moroccan Bath 120Dh, Massage 180Dh | Al-Bateen | 32nd Street, opposite BMW | tel. 02 6 65 57 07 | www.orientalspauae.com*

INSIDER TIP DESERT FROM ABOVE

One of the loveliest ways of experiencing the desert close up is by taking a hot-air balloon flight over the sea and the dunes. The five-hour trip starts at 5.30am in Abu Dhabi (city), followed by a one-hour drive to Al Ain, where the balloons lift off. After the balloon flight guests are brought back to Abu Dhabi. *Sept–May, 880 Dh (children 750) | tel. 04 2 48 54 9 49 | www.ballooning.ae*

ENTERTAINMENT

INSIDER TIP AL-DHAFRA

This dhow runs dinner cruises (Arabian fish and steak dishes) along the Corniche, with views of the capital's skyline. *Daily 8pm–10.30pm | 150Dh | Al-Mina, between the Iranian Market and the Fish Market | tel. 02 6 73 22 66 | www.aldhafra.net*

G-CLUB

A nightclub with a large dance floor, G-Club offers reggae and soul, salsa and R&B. Saturday is ladies' night. *Daily 10pm–3am | Le Royal Meridien hotel | Nadja Street (6th Street), Tourist Club Area | tel. 02 6 44 66 66 | www.lemeridien abudhabi.com*

INSIDER TIP PEARLS AND CAVIAR ☼

Abu Dhabi's most spectacular bar is part of the Shangri-La hotel. A must for design lovers is the chill-out area on the ● roof terrace, with its white lounge furniture and black-and-white marble. It has spectacular views of the Arabian Gulf and Sheikh Zayed Mosque, which is lit up like a palace. *Daily | Qaryat al-Beri, Between the Bridges | tel. 02 5 09 88 88 | www.shangri-la.com*

ROCK BOTTOM CAFÉ

Different theme nights and events are held each day. The music includes hip-hop and R&B. *Daily noon–3am | Al-Diar Capital Hotel, 2nd Floor | Meena Street | tel. 02 6 78 77 00*

WHERE TO STAY

AL-DIAR MINA

Has medium-range accommodation near the eastern Corniche. Also popular with new residents, who often book the rooms with kitchen facilities on a weekly

There are views of the Arabian Gulf from the pools of the Hilton

or monthly basis. *106 rooms and apartments | Al-Mina Street, corner Salam Street | tel. 02 6 78 10 00 | www.aldiar hotels.com | Moderate*

AL-DIAR REGENCY
Offers a central location near the eastern Corniche, small rooms with cooking facilities, plus a fitness area. Inexpensive accommodation. *193 rooms | Al-Meena Street, corner Al-Salam Street | tel. 02 6 76 50 00 | www.aldiarhotels.com | Budget–Moderate*

EMIRATES PALACE
This magnificent fairytale palace is a 7-star luxury beach hotel with 1.3km (0.8mi) of imported sand (from North Africa). Guests can easily get lost in all the identical halls and corridors, decorated with marble, gold and stucco, but one of the 1500 smiling employees will always be happy to help. *394 rooms | Corniche Road West | tel. 02 6 90 90 00 | www. emiratespalace.com | Expensive*

HILTON
Separated from the beach by the waterfront promenade and with views of Breakwater, the Hilton has large rooms with comfortable furniture and luxury touches, including a coffee maker. Guests have access to the Hiltonia Beach Club opposite, offering 350m (380yds) of private beach, shaded by palm trees, as well as wellness and sports facilities. *388 rooms | Corniche Road West | tel. 02 6 81 19 00 | www.hilton.com | Expensive*

SABA
Medium-range accommodation in a central location. Rooms have air conditioning, a television and a fridge, and there are two Indian restaurants and two nightclubs. *54 rooms | 10th Street | Al-Meena | tel. 02 6 44 83 33 | Budget*

SANDS
Comfortable hotel with six restaurants, a large fitness area, a rooftop pool and transfer to the Beach Club. *253 rooms | Sheikh Zayed the Second Street (Electra Street) | tel. 02 6 15 66 66 | www.sands-hotel-abudhabi.com | Moderate*

SHANGRI-LA ☆
After Emirates Palace, this is the city's most beautiful hotel. Constructed in

of the health club. Facilities include two large pools, a shopping street in the style of a modern Arabian souk and an excellent spa centre offering a great range of treatments. *214 rooms | Qaryat al-Beri, Between the Bridges | tel. 02 5 09 88 88 | www.shangri-la.com | Expensive*

INFORMATION

ABU DHABI TOURISM AUTHORITY
Maqta Fort, Maqta Bridge | tel. 02 4 44 04 44 | www.visitabudhabi.ae

WHERE TO GO

LIWA OASES ●
(125 E–F 5–6) (*E–G 9–10*)

playful Arabian style on the mainland, opposite the island capital, it resembles a palace from 'The Arabian Nights'. The view over the water towards the Grand Mosque on the other side is particularly lovely, especially from the outdoor pool

Surrounded by desert and high, shimmering sand dunes as far as the eye can see, the Liwa Oases are a collection of about 40 villages, located around 230km (142mi) southwest of Abu Dhabi

BOOKS & FILMS

▶ **Arabian Sands** – an exciting account by British explorer and travel writer Wilfred Thesiger about his crossing of the Rub al-Khali, the 'Empty Quarter', in the years 1947–1950

▶ **The Emirates – A Natural History** – there is much more to the desert than sand, as this illustrated reference book (2005), edited by Peter Hellyer and Simon Aspinall, makes clear

▶ **Filling in the Blanks** – a record of archaeological excavations in Abu Dhabi by Peter Hellyer on behalf of the Abu Dhabi Islands Archaeological Survey

▶ **The Merchants** – an account by Michael Field of how society has evolved since the discovery of oil, by tracing the history of the region's most prominent families (2005)

▶ **Sheikh Zayed Life and Times 1918–2004** – a photographic history of the first president of the UAE by well-known UAE photographer Noor Ali Rashid

▶ **Syriana** – this political thriller (2005, directed by Stephen Gagan) starting George Clooney and Matt Damon is about oil. Dubai and the emirates with their unique desert landscape provide the setting

city. They stretch for more than 100km (62mi) in an arc along the edge of the famous Rub al-Khali (Empty Quarter), from Hamim in the east to Arrada in the west. The oases have been inhabited by the tribe of the Bani Yas since the 16th century. In the 1940s they were visited by the British explorer Wilfred Thesiger, who recorded his travels in his book 'Arabian Sands'. These days a large section of the population are from Asia, and the introduction of modern agricultural machinery makes working in the date palm plantations and vegetable fields easier. But the villages (population approx. 90,000) still have a tranquil atmosphere, owing to their isolation. For that reason the Liwa Oases are still the best place in the Emirates to experience the magnificent beauty and the spiritual qualities of the Arabian desert *(see chapter Excursions & Tours, p. 97)*.

One accommodation option that lives up to its magnificent desert setting is ● Qasr al-Sarab *(205 rooms | Hanim | Qasr al Sarab Road | tel. 02 8 86 20 88 | www.qasralsarab.anantara.com | Expensive)*. The resort is among Abu Dhabi's loveliest hotels; its remote location amid the sand dunes and its stunning design are exceptional. It is built in a genuine Arabian style, executed with incredible attention to detail. The room sizes start at 40sq m (430sq ft), and the hotel's restaurants combine outstanding food with a romantic desert ambience. The leisure programme includes desert tours in four-by-fours or by camel, and the Anantara Spa is superb. Early risers will enjoy the 'nature walks' through the desert.

SIR BANI YAS ★ ☺
(124 B–C 1–2) (*ʘ C 6*)
The 87sq km (33sq mi) island of Sir Bani Yas, 8km (5mi) from the Jebel Dhanna

peninsula, has been turned into a wildlife reserve. The island has been inhabited for 2000 years, and in the 7th century was populated by Christians. Mangroves, steppe, bush, desert and freshwater ponds make up the landscape between the 150-m (490ft) mountains *(sir = stony plateau)*, and some 3 million plants and trees have been specially planted. Sheikh Zayed introduced oryx and other antelopes, deer, giraffes, hyenas, gazelles, emus and other fauna, and today the reserve, previously his private island, is home to an estimated 30,000 animals). A ☺ hotel of the Anantara chain, renowned in Asia, was opened in 2008 and offers environmentally friendly living in a luxurious rustic desert style as well as beach and wildlife experiences: *Islands Resort & Spa (64 rooms | tel. 02 8 01 54 00 | www.desertislands.anantara. com | 250km (156mi) west of the city of Abu Dhabi)*.

AL-AIN

(127 E–F 1–2) (*ʘ K 6*) **This modern oasis (population: 440,000) is a large garden city, traversed by four-lane roads with countless roundabouts, but it also has many lushly-planted, flower-filled green spaces, including two dozen parks.** Situated 160km (100 mi) east of Abu Dhabi, at the foot of Jebel Hafeet (1,348m/4,442ft), Al Ain is the emirate's agricultural centre, thanks to its plentiful water supply. As the birthplace of Sheikh Zayed, it was developed and turned into a showpiece. As recently as the 1970s it consisted of just a handful of villages grouped around the freshwater springs, and its inhabitants made their living from the date palms. Today archaeologists are researching the Bronze Age settlements in the surrounding area and

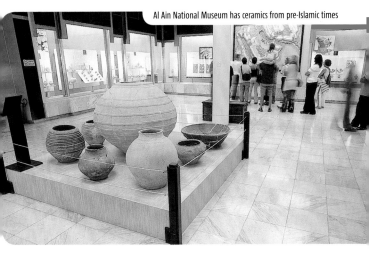

WHERE TO START?
Coming from Dubai or Abu Dhabi drive down Khalifa Bin Zayed Street and turn right into Al Ain Street to the **Clock Tower**. Park there and walk down Al Ain Street to Al Ain Palace Museum. Walk straight through Al Ain Oasis to get to Al Ain Fort and Al Ain National Museum.

young locals study at the UAE University. The modern city has also opened up to tourism.

SIGHTSEEING

AL AIN FORT

Al Ain Fort (also known as Sultan Fort or Eastern Fort) is next to the National Museum. It was built in 1910 by Sheikh Sultan al-Nahyan (the father of the first president of the United Arab Emirates, Sheikh Zayed). It has a square floor plan with round towers, and was originally built out of sun-dried clay bricks. A few rooms of the restored fort have been turned into a museum, while the courtyard is used for events. *Daily 8am–noon and 4pm–6pm | free entry | Omar Bin al-Khatab Road*

AL-AIN NATIONAL MUSEUM ★

This is the best and most significant museum of the oasis. The 5000-year-old Hili exhibits are a unique treasure. If you have to choose between the archaeological excavation site *(see p. 46)* and the museum, because of too little time to visit both, you should opt for this museum. Located next to Al Ain Fort, it displays discoveries from the Bronze Age to the Islamic present from the Hili Archaeological Park and Jebel Hafeet. There are also ethnographic exhibits, Bedouin jewellery and photographs on the development of the oil industry. The state gifts to Sheikh Zayed, who died in 2004, seem by contrast a bit on the strange side! *Sat–Thu 8am–7pm, Fri 3pm–7.30pm | entry 3Dh | Omar Bin al-Khatab Road | www.adach.ae*

Al Ain National Museum has ceramics from pre-Islamic times

AL-AIN OASIS ● ☺

Dense palm gardens, irrigated by water brought by stone falaj channels, give the oasis next to the museum's entrance a peaceful atmosphere. A network of paths, along which are a few small mosques, made of clay, wind through the oasis, and the vegetable fields and palm tree groves are surrounded by low walls. The contemplative atmosphere, the lush vegetation and the sense of a bygone age make the oasis a joy for every walker. *Al-Ain Oasis | Centre*

AL-AIN PALACE MUSEUM

This former palace of the ruling family has been restored and converted into a museum to document the life and family of Sheikh Zayed. Enjoy a coffee and some dates in a large dewaniya tent. *Sun–Thu 9am–7.30pm, Fri 3pm–8pm | free entry | Sanaya Road (western edge of Al Ain Oasis)*

AL-AIN ZOO

This zoo is also a great place for a relaxing walk in a wonderfully landscaped environment: between savannah grass, palm trees and large ponds, 4000 animals are at home on 850ha (2000 acres), including lions, antelopes, crocodiles, gorillas and giant tortoises. There's a cafeteria and refreshment stalls, and every evening there is a humorously interpreted INSIDER TIP bird and animal show (free). *Daily 8am–8pm | entry 15Dh | Zoo R/A, Zayed Al-Awwal/Nahyan Al-Awwal Street*

INSIDER TIP AL-JAHILI FORT

Impressively battlemented, with two massive, round towers and a formidable wooden gate, the largest fort in town was built by Sheikh Zayed Bin Khalifa in 1898. The main tower rises up in four levels, which taper towards the top. Sheikh Zayed was born in the fort in 1918; he became the charismatic head of state of the UAE until his death in 2004, and his portrait can be seen everywhere in Al Ain. The fort also has a photographic exhibition of the works of Sir Wilfred Thesiger, the British traveller and desert explorer who, in 1945, began his crossing of the Rub al-Khali (Empty Quarter). *Sat–Thu 8am–6pm, Fri 3pm–8pm | free entry | Al-Ain Street | Al-Jahili | www.adach.ae*

CAMEL MARKET ★

There is a pungent smell of camels in the air at the Emirates' last big camel market, situated on the outskirts of town. The animals, which are kept in enclosures in a large compound, are not expensive racing camels but sold for meat, milk and breeding, with some young camels on display too. You can try some camel milk in exchange for a tip. The mood at the market is ribald and friendly; if you want to take pictures, ask permission first and give the Pakistani keepers some baksheesh. *Daily 7am–1pm | free entry | Wadi Al Ain Road, southeast of town on the road towards Ibri and Nizwa*

HILI ARCHAEOLOGICAL PARK ★

The park, also known as *Hili Gardens*, was created around a restored tomb dating back to around 2700 BC (Hili Tomb). There are several ancient tombs as well as the remains of a Bronze Age settlement. The sensation here is the Grand Tomb, which is more than 4000 years old and has a diameter of 10m (32ft). It is one of the last remains of the mysterious Umm al-Nar culture, which started the region's first major era of civilisation, between 3000 BC and 2000 BC. The centre of the civilisation was here in Hili. Discoveries from the site are on display in the Al-Ain National Museum *(see p. 45)*. *Sat–Thu 4pm–10pm, Fri 10am–10pm |*

entry 3Dh | Arz al-Bahar Street, from Mo-
hammed Bin Khalifa Road | 10km (6mi)
north towards Dubai | www.adach.ae

FOOD & DRINK

AL-DIWAN

Serves Lebanese and Iranian cuisine as well as fish dishes and a large selection of shellfish. This is where many Arab expatriates meet in a lively atmosphere.

HUT CAFÉ

This comfortable café is a great place to relax from breakfast onwards. It serves cakes and snacks such as crêpes, salads and soups as well as a large selection of sandwiches. *Daily | Khalifa Street | tel. 03 7 51 65 26| Budget*

THE WOK

One of the best restaurants in town, the Wok offers oriental and Asian cuisine, fish

There's a jocular, friendly atmosphere at the Camel Market

Daily | Khalifa Street, near Union Bank | tel. 03 7 64 44 45 | Moderate

GOLDEN FORK

Diners are greeted with a refreshing towel, a welcoming soup and water, and then invited to order from the Filipino menu, which includes sweet-and-sour vegetables and grilled seafood. Serves inexpensive, good food, and has an internet corner on the first floor. *Daily | Khalifa Street | tel. 03 7 66 03 36 | Budget*

and seafood buffets, changing culinary theme nights, and has a separate sushi bar. *Daily | Hotel Intercontinental | Khalid Ibn Sultan Street | tel. 03 7 68 66 86 | www.intercontinental.com | Expensive*

SHOPPING

AL-AIN MALL

Some 200 shops (only some of which are internationally known brands) and two dozen cafés and restaurants on three floors (including a food court) make this a great place to shop or window-shop. Entertainment includes an ice rink and a few attractions for children. *Sat–Wed 10am–10pm, Thu / Fri 10am–11pm | Al-Falaheya Street | Kuwaitat | www.alainmall.net*

WHERE TO STAY

AL-AIN ROTANA
This member of a 5-star chain popular throughout the UAE is the best establishment in Al Ain, with nice rooms, newly designed in 2008, as well as poolside chalets and villas, and a convenient central location. It serves an excellent breakfast buffet, and in the evening tour groups rub shoulders with locals in its restaurants, which are known for their good food. *198 rooms | Sheikh Zayed Bin Sultan Street | tel. 03 7545111 | www.rotana.com | Expensive*

CITY SEASONS
This three-storey modern, mid-range hotel has a gym, a pool and a health club, and offers ayurveda massages, internet in the rooms and spacious suites. *48 rooms | Khalifa Street | Mowijai | tel. 03 7550220 | www.cityseasonsalain. com | Budget*

GREEN MUBAZZARAH CHALETS
This is where the locals come to relax: in smart, newly built chalets, luxuriously equipped, 13km (8mi) south of town, at the foot of Jebel Hafeet, between palm trees, mountains and bare rocks. Guests can enjoy well-tended gardens and parks as well as the hot springs (separate pools for men and women with spring water for skin and joint problems). You can either cook for yourself or eat in the re-

FESTIVALS IN ABU DHABI

Culture has been a major focus for quite a few years now in Abu Dhabi. Saadiyat is being developed as an 'Island of Culture' with several new cultural museums being built over the next few years. The emirate is also keen to encourage cultural festivals. In February the Goethe Institute puts on the *Heritage Film Festival* in the Heritage Village, during which three films on the same theme but from different countries are screened each evening; afterwards they are discussed by the directors, actors and critics. *(4 days at the end of February | www. goethe.de/gulfregion | free entry)*

At the *Gourmet Festival* in Abu Dhabi city award-winning chefs from east and west run all kinds of culinary events, from cooking classes to royal dinners, and all the large hotels serve specialities from around the world. One of the highlights of the festival is the celebrity dinner, held in one of the top hotels. Hosted by a celebrity chef, it is a celebration of top-quality food and wine. *First two weeks in February | www. gourmetabudhabi.ae | Information and bookings: Abu Dhabi Tourism Authority*

The *Abu Dhabi Grand Prix*, a Formula 1 race, has been held on Yas Island since 2009. The track, rated as spectacular by car racing fans, was designed by the German circuit designer Herman Tielke; it runs very close to the harbour in places (Yas Marina Circuit) as well as under a bridge that forms part of Yas Hotel. After the race top-class *pop and rock concerts* are held. *Early–mid-November | www.abudhabi-grand-prix.com*

Jebel Hafeet is the highest mountain in the emirate of Abu Dhabi

sort's restaurant. *200 Chalets | Jebel Hafeet Road | tel. 03 7 83 95 55 | Moderate*

MERCURE GRAND JEBEL HAFEET ☆

Located at a height of 915m (3000ft), on the winding road up Jebel Hafeet (15km/9mi south of Al Ain), is this midrange establishment with views of the mountains from the rooms. *124 rooms | Jebel Hafeet Road | tel. 03 7 83 88 88 | www.mercure.com | Moderate*

INFORMATION

Al Ain Municipality | Ali bin Abu Taleb Street | tel. 03 7 64 20 00 | www.alain.ae

WHERE TO GO

JEBEL HAFEET (127 F2) *(ⓜ K 6–7)*
15km (9mi) south of the town of Al Ain, a 12-km (7.5mi) road twists up 60 hairpin bends all the way to the top of the 1348-m (4442ft) Jebel Hafeet, the highest mountain in the emirate of Abu Dhabi *(also see the chapter Excursions & Tours p. 97).*

BURAIMI OASIS (127 F1) *(ⓜ K 6)*
The oasis of Buraimi was once an important stopover for caravans; it is in Oman and lies to the northeast of Al Ain. It's just a 5-km (3mi) trip from Al Ain's centre. You currently need a visa to visit Oman, but this can be obtained at the border crossing.

The interesting al-Khandaq fort on the main road has massive corner towers, impeccably restored with great attention to detail *(Sat–Thu 8am–6pm, Fri 8am–noon and 4pm–6pm | free entry).* Haggling is part of the fun at the covered souk next to the fort, which sells food, spices and also souvenirs. Behind the souk is a date palm oasis with narrow paths flanked by clay walls. The palm trees are supplied with water via a traditional falaj system.

One magnificent example of sacred architecture is the nearby Sultan Qaboos Mosque; its two slender minarets tower above a wonderful green dome.

DUBAI

With its 7-star hotels, tallest building in the world, artificial islands and the largest water park in the Middle East, Dubai is known for doing things on a grand scale. On its hunt for new records, the emirate has become a kind of world wonder in its own right.

Dubai is the extravagant commercial and business centre of the Middle East, a distribution hub for goods, money and services, and it is also the most significant of the seven emirates from a tourism perspective. Income from international tourism has ended its dependency on oil. With the creation of artificial islands in the Arabian Gulf off the coast of Dubai, as well as massive property projects in the sea, city and desert, the emirate (population: 1.7 million) has also been a gigantic building site for years. The sheikhdom now extends 40km (25mi) to the south, all the way to Jebel Ali, and to Dubailand in the east, with almost all of its inhabitants living in this area.

The discovery of oil helped the emirate, which has a size of 3900sq km (1500sq mi) and consists largely of desert, leap into the modern era in the 1960s.

Dubai was founded in around 1830, when an ancestor of the ruling al-Maktoum family moved to Dubai Creek. After the British signed several contracts with the tribal leaders from 1835 onwards, to protect their trade routes to India, Iranian and Indian merchants moved to the Creek. The emirate is highly multicultural these days: you will encounter people from more than 120 nations in Dubai.

Photo: Dubai Marina Yacht Club

Mega-city and cosmopolitan commercial port – utopian construction projects and playground for the super-rich

WHERE TO START?
The starting point of a city tour is the Creek, the waterway dividing Dubai. Wander from the **Sheraton Dubai Creek Hotel** *(Metro Union Square)* on the waterfront towards the sea and cross from Deira to Bur Dubai in an *abra*. Walk through the shop-filled streets to Dubai Museum in Al Fahidi-Fort and to the historic Bastakiya quarter.

At just 10 percent of the population, the proud locals are now a minority in their own country.

DUBAI (CITY)

MAP IN THE BACK COVER
(122 C4) *(𝔐 J 4)* **With its luxury shopping malls, beaches and man-made islands, this historic trading port on the Creek has become the largest city in the United Arab Emirates and a glam-**

orous international holiday destination.
Arabian souks and modern shopping
centres make Dubai a shoppers' paradise, while sandy beaches drenched in
year-round sunshine attract beach-lovers.

Dubai's landmark: Burj Al Arab

With hotels to suit every budget, everyone can experience the dynamic city and
its attractions.

If you spend time on the Creek, Dubai's
traditional lifeline, it seems as if nothing
much has changed: fat-bellied dhows,
arriving heavily laden from Iran and India, are moored next to Al-Khor Corniche,
Dubai's waterfront promenade. To the
south of the strait is Bur Dubai, with the
historical fort and emir's palace; to the
north is Deira, with a mix of modern
skyscrapers, older buildings and oriental souks. Bridges and tunnels connect
the various parts of the city. Towards
the south Sheikh Zayed Road is lined by
architecturally striking skyscrapers, while
Jumeirah Road, which runs along the
beach, is lined by luxurious beach hotels,
making it the tourist domain. This is the
location of the Burj-al-Arab hotel, the
most expensive hotel in the world, which
was considered Dubai's boldest construction project until just a few years ago. But
that is no longer the case. The World is
currently being constructed on artificial
islands shaped like a palm – refuges for
the rich who are demonstrating that everything is possible in Dubai.

SIGHTSEEING

BURJ AL ARAB ★

The best-known hotel in the world, the
'Arabian Tower', was built on an artificial
island off the beach in 1999. Dubai's
landmark rises 321m (1053ft) into the
air, billowing its dhow-shaped sails of
concrete and glass. To visit the hotel, it
is necessary to make a reservation in
one of the cafés, restaurants or bars
(240–550Dh per person). You will be
given a reservation number for the front
entrance after handing over your credit
card details. Alternatively, you can book
a sightseeing tour through one of the

travel agencies. *Jumeirah Beach Road | tel. 04 3 01 76 00 and 043 01 77 77 | Metro: First Gulf Bank*

BURJ KHALIFA ⭐

Visible from almost everywhere, the tallest building in the world was completed in 2009. The 828-m (2716ft) tower houses apartments, offices and hotels, including the Armani hotel. The viewing platform 'At the Top' is located on the tower's 124th floor, at a height of 442m (1450ft). Tickets are available from the At the Top desk in Dubai Mall. A moving walkway will take you to Burj Khalifa and into a double-storey elevator that takes visitors non-stop to the visitors' deck in just one minute. Tickets for a direct visit cost 400Dh, while for a later, reserved visit they are 100Dh *(children up to the age of 12, 75Dh)*. *Sun–Wed 10am–10pm, Thu–Sat 10am–midnight | Doha Street | from Sheikh Zayed Road 1st Interchange (Defence R/A) | www.burjdubai.com | Metro: Dubai Mall/Burj Khalifa*

DHOW CRUISE

One way of getting an attractive view of old and new Dubai is by taking a cruise in an Arabian dhow on the Creek, the body of water that divides the city. *Daily 11.30am, 1.30pm, 2.30pm, 3.30pm, 5.30pm | duration 1hr, 45Dh | Dinner Cruise 8.30pm, duration 2hrs, 225Dh incl. hotel transfers | Saeef Road (from the British Embassy) | Bur Dubai | tel. 04 3 36 84 07 | www.tour-dubai. com | Metro: Saeediya*

DUBAI FOUNTAIN ●

With its artistic installation of water fountains shooting high up into the air, dancing to the rhythm of classical music, Dubai Lake, at the base of Burj Khalifa, delights passers-by several times each hour. It is spectacular after dark, when vivid colour is thrown into the mix. *Dubai Mall | Financial Centre Road | from Sheikh Zayed Road, 1st Interchange | Metro: Dubai Mall*

DUBAI MUSEUM ⭐

A lesson in history and regional knowledge, this unique museum, located in the historic premises of the old fort and a modern underground wing, provides a comprehensive insight into what life and culture in Dubai were like in the past. Millennia-old discoveries from the region's few excavation sites are presented in an engaging way, using modern technology and multimedia shows, and are interesting even for those who usually shy away from history museums. *Sat–*

MARCO POLO HIGHLIGHTS

⭐ **Burj Al Arab**
A monument in the sea and still Dubai's most famous landmark
→ p. 52

⭐ **Burj Khalifa**
The tallest building in the world – a marvel not just from the outside → p. 53

⭐ **Dubai Museum**
The history and life of the city, on display in the old fort of the ruling family → p. 53

⭐ **Aquaventure**
Located on Palm Jumeirah, the largest and most exciting water-park on the Arabian Gulf really is an experience → p. 56

⭐ **Atlantis**
A dream in pink, this themed hotel at the tip of Palm Jumeirah also houses a spectacular aquarium → p. 58

Thu 8.30am–8pm, Fri 3pm–9pm | entry 3Dh | Al-Fahidi Street | Al-Fahidi Fort | Bur Dubai | Metro: Saeediya

HERITAGE

Camels, henna painting, pearl diving and wind tower houses are brought to life in these two museum villages focusing on the architectural and maritime traditions of the region. Visit after sunset, when

the extravagant Jumeirah Mosque is an exception. The Sheikh Mohammed Centre for Cultural Understanding runs **INSIDER TIP** one-hour guided tours of the mosque *(meet on Sat, Sun, Tue, Thu outside the mosque, opposite The One furniture store; registering starts at 9am, guided tours 10am–11.15am, 10Dh)*. Men have to wear long trousers, women are given a black *abaya* and a scarf to cover

Invitingly illuminated, Jumeirah Mosque is also open to non-Muslims

the locals come here, too, creating a lively atmosphere. *Sat–Thu 8am–10pm, Fri 8am–11am and 3pm–10pm | free entry | Shindagha Road | Bur-Dubai side of the Creek estuary | Metro: Al Ghubaiba*

JUMEIRAH MOSQUE

This ivory-coloured mosque, dating from 1983, in playful Arabian architecture with a double minaret and a domed roof supported by columns, is illuminated by thousands of tiny lights at the onset of darkness. Non-Muslims are not normally permitted to enter Dubai's mosques, but

themselves. *Jumeirah Beach Road | www. cultures.ae | Metro: Trade Centre*

THE PALM JUMEIRAH

It is easy to take a look around the 4-km (2.5mi) artificial island, with its mansions, hotels, restaurants, shops and yacht-filled marina. **INSIDER TIP** A *Monorail* runs from the coastal station 'Gateway' at the Royal Mirage hotel via Palm Jumeirah all the way to Atlantis hotel; it stops twice on the way *(15Dh, return 25Dh)*.

FOOD & DRINK

INSIDERTIP BASTA ARTS CAFÉ

This Arabian-cum-Mediterranean garden restaurant, in one of the restored buildings of the Bastakiya quarter, offers salads, soups, delicious juices and peppermint tea – a stylish way to take a break while strolling around the city. *Daily | Al-Fahidi Street 63, Al-Fahidi R/A | tel. 04 3 53 50 71 | Moderate | Metro: Saeediya*

LUCKY

Indian, Chinese and Mongolian dishes at inexpensive prices are served in a clean environment. Try the delicious *alu mutter* and *palak paneer*, two vegetarian Indian dishes, and *chicken tikka*. *Daily | Al-Fahidi Street | Meena Bazar | Bur Dubai | tel. 04 3 53 45 63 | Budget | Metro: Saeediya*

PIERCHIC ⌫

A 100-m (130yds) wooden pier runs from Madinat Jumeirah to this fish restaurant in the sea, serving top-quality seafood with an Asian twist. Views of Burj Al Arab and the glittering city skyline add to the experience. Outdoor tables have to be booked a day in advance. *Daily | Madinat Jumeirah | Umm Suqeim | tel. 04 3 66 88 88 | www.madinatjumeirah.com | Metro: First Gulf Bank | Expensive*

SEZZAM ⌫

With views of the 'winter wonderland' of Ski Dubai, diners in this huge restaurant order dishes prepared in and served from open kitchens: fish and meat dishes, baked, roasted, steamed or fried. Attracts a young, sophisticated clientele. *Daily | Sheikh Zayed Road | Kempinski-Hotel | Mall of the Emirates | tel. 04 3 413 600 | www.sezzam.com | Moderate | Metro: Mall of the Emirates*

SHOPPING

In addition to some 40 luxurious shopping malls, in which international-brand clothes, cosmetics, shoes and electronic goods are sold, souks and open shopping streets, with lots of small shops, deliver authentic Arabian atmosphere. Souks that are particularly worth visiting are the *Gold Souk (Sikkat al-Khail Street, Deira)*, next to the ● *Spice Souk*, where saffron and cinnamon are sold out of open jute sacks, and the *Perfume Souk (Sikkat al-Khail Street, Deira)*, where fragrances are created and sold.

DUBAI MALL ●

This mall, which opened in 2008, has more than 1200 shops as well as the ● *Dubai Aquarium* (see 20,000 fish and other marine creatures through a viewing window measuring 33m x 8m / 108ft x 26ft) or from inside a tunnel) and a large ice rink. *Daily 10am–midnight | Doha Street | from Sheikh Zayed Road, 1st Interchange | www.thedubaimall.com | Metro: Dubai Mall*

INSIDERTIP KINOKINUYA

A paradise for book-lovers, this branch of the Japanese chain resembles an enormous library, with books on subjects ranging from landscape design to Buddhism, as well as novels, coffee table books and paperbacks. *Daily 10am–midnight | Dubai Mall | Financial Centre Road | from Sheikh Zayed Road | 1st Interchange | Metro: Dubai Mall*

THE MALL OF THE EMIRATES

This huge mall contains 466 upmarket shops and boutiques, including a branch of the upmarket British department store Harvey Nichols. *Sun–Wed 10am–10pm, Thu–Sat 10am–midnight | Sheikh Zayed Road | between Interchange 4 and 5 |*

www.malloftheemirates.com | Metro: Mall of the Emirates

SOUK MADINAT JUMEIRAH ●

An upmarket version of a bazaar, this replica of a traditional souk is part of a complex operated by three luxury hotels, which are connected by waterways. In addition to 75 small shops there are lots

ends. *Daily 10am–6pm | 200Dh | Jumeirah Road | The Palm Jumeirah | Atlantis Resort, Crescent Road | www.atlantisthepalm.com | Metro: Nakheel*

SKI DUBAI ●

Dubai's winter wonderland is a snowy world in which artificial snow falls only at night, creating constantly ideal con-

Skiing in the desert? Ski Dubai in the Mall of Emirates makes it possible

of cafés and restaurants. *Daily 9am–midnight | Madinat Jumeirah | Umm Suqeim | www.madinatjumeirah.com | Metro: Mall of the Emirates*

SPORTS & ACTIVITIES

AQUAVENTURE ★

This waterpark belonging to the Atlantis Resort is located on the tip of The Palm Jumeirah. It is packed with thrilling water slides and rides. Seven of the slides start from the 30-m (98ft) 'Ziggurat' tower. Or you can float along a 2.3km (1.5mi) channel on a large rubber ring. There are waiting times for the attractions at week-

ditions for winter sports. The indoor ski arena has five pistes and descents of up to 400m (1300ft), guaranteeing plenty of fun. There is even a chairlift and a ski hut serving hot chocolate. *Daily 10am–11pm | entry 2hrs 180Dh, full day 300Dh incl. equipment, 120Dh for the Snow Park | Sheikh Zayed Road, 4th Interchange | The Mall of the Emirates | tel. 04 4 09 41 00 | www.skidxb.com | Metro: Mall of the Emirates*

WATERBUS ●

There are four waterbus routes on the Creek, between Bur Dubai, Sabkha (Deira), Beniyas (Deira) and See (Creek

Park), costing 4Dh per short-distance trip. **INSIDER TIP** The longest (tourist) route between Shindagha (Heritage Village) and Seef (25 mins) costs 25Dh return. *Daily 8am–midnight*

ENTERTAINMENT

THE AGENCY

Dark, modern and with a mix of Asia and the Middle East, The Agency attracts business people for after work drinks at the high cocktail tables. Choose between 500 wines, 70 of which are served by the glass; afterwards there is dinner and dancing upstairs. *Daily noon–midnight | Sheikh Zayed Road | Emirates Towers Shopping Boulevard | tel. 04 33 00 00 | www.jumeirahemiratestowers.com | Metro: Emirates Towers*

PLAN B

A nightclub with a popular bar, changing DJs and live music on Thursdays. *Daily 10pm–3am | Wafi City |Oud Metha | tel. 04 3 24 47 77 | Metro: Oud Metha*

INSIDER TIP ROCK BOTTOM CAFÉ

Bar with Harley-Davidson memorabilia for motorbike and rock fans; live rock music starts at 10pm. *Daily noon–3am | Trade Centre Road (opposite Burjuman) | Regent Palace Hotel | Bur Dubai | tel. 04 3 96 38 88 | Metro: Khalid Bin Al Waleed*

SCARLETT'S BAR

This nightclub with live performances attracts a hip audience of European and Australian expatriates. The lively atmosphere continues after midnight, when the DJ plays the latest hits. *Daily noon–3am | Sheikh Zayed Road | Emirates Towers Shopping Boulevard, ground floor | tel. 04 3 19 80 88 | www.jumeirah emiratestowers.com | Metro: Emirates Towers*

WHERE TO STAY

AL-KHALEEJ

Although the beaches are a taxi ride away, this mid-range hotel has a great city location, and the best rooms (with a balcony) have views of the Creek. In the evenings, guests are catered for by an Italian restaurant and a popular bar. *105 rooms | Al-Nasser Square | Deira | tel. 04 2 211 44 | www.alkhaleejhotels.com | Moderate | Metro: Baniyas Square*

LOW BUDGET

▶ Every *'harbour trip'* from Deira to Bur Dubai on the other side of the Creek (and vice versa) costs just 1Dh, in an abra.

▶ The food in *Flavours restaurant* is good and inexpensive. The view of the Creek from the 🌿 terrace is free. *Twin Towers, 3rd floor | Baniyas Road | Deira | tel. 04 2 21 41 12 | Metro: Baniyas Square*

▶ The performances and folklore shows in the *Heritage & Diving Village (see p. 54)* can be visited for free.

▶ The view from 'At the Top', on the 124th floor of Burj Khalifa costs 400Dh; get a similar ● view from the bar Neos on the 63rd floor of 'The Address' hotel opposite, which will only cost you the price of a drink.

▶ Dubai Mall runs a ● free shuttle bus from various hotels to the shopping mall – a somewhat alternative city tour!

ATLANTIS ⭐

This hotel on The Palm Jumeirah, opened in 2008, is a spectacular pink hotel with maritime decoration and turrets – construction cost 1.5 billion US dollars. It has 17 restaurants and bars, a waterpark with a shark pool and many aquariums (visible from some of the suites). The monorail goes to this luxury hotel, but only hotel guests are allowed into the lobby. You can access the Lost Chambers Aquarium via the hotel's own shopping complex *(entry 100Dh). 1539 rooms | Crescent Road | The Palm Jumeirah | tel. 04 4261000 | www.atlantisthepalm. com | Expensive*

GOLDEN SANDS

The rooms and apartments (with one to three bedrooms) in nine buildings on the outskirts of Bur Dubai are decorated in a modern, utilitarian manner, with a kitchenette, and are popular with families. There is a breakfast restaurant, a pool on the roof terrace, in-house car rental and a travel agency. *950 rooms | Al-Mankhool Road | tel. 04 3555553 | www.goldensandsdubai.com | Moderate | Metro: Saeediya, Al-Karama*

MEENA PLAZA

This little bit of India in Dubai is a nine-storey establishment in a smart shopping mall near the Burjuman Centre. In addition to a restaurant with Indian cuisine there are also two bars and a coffee shop as well as INSIDER TIP an ayurveda centre. Free airport transfers. *82 rooms | Al-Mankhool Road (next to Choitrams) | Bur Dubai | tel. 04 3514222 | www. meenaplazahotel.20m.com | Budget | Metro: Khalid Bin Al Waleed*

NOVA

Between Indian restaurants and oriental shopping streets in the older neighbour-hood of Bur Dubai, the Nova is a good choice for those who like to be in the midst of things or enjoy shopping in the more individual stores. It has an internet corner in the foyer. *84 rooms | Al-Fahidi Street | Meena Bazar | Bur Dubai | tel. 04 3559000 | www.dubainovahotel.com | Budget | Metro: Saeediya*

ONE AND ONLY ROYAL MIRAGE ●

For sun, sand, sea and luxury, the Royal Mirage, one of Dubai's nicest hotels, is in the style of an oriental palace, furnished with antiques, filled with flowers and with rooms in a smart, modern design with an Arabian twist. After sunset lights transform the patios and palm tree gardens into a romantic paradise. *450 rooms in 3 buildings | Al Sufouh Road | tel. 04 3999999 | www.oneandonlyresorts. com | Expensive | Metro: Nakheel*

THE PALACE

This opulent city hotel in the oriental style is located on an artificial lake in the immediate vicinity of shopping malls and

the Burj Khalifa. The smartly designed rooms have luxurious bathrooms; the pool complex is surrounded by palm trees, and there is a wonderful spa. *242 rooms | Burj Khalifa Boulevard | The Old Town | tel. 04 4 28 78 88 | www.thepalace-dubai. com | Expensive | Metro: Dubai Mall*

INFORMATION

DUBAI DEPARTMENT OF TOURISM & COMMERCE MARKETING
With Welcome stalls in the airport (24 hrs) and in the shopping malls Deira City, Burjuman, Hamarain, Wafi and Mercato (all *10am–10pm*). *NBD-Bldg. (National Bank of Dubai), 10th Floor | Dubai | tel. 04 2 23 00 00 | www.dubaitourism.com*

WHERE TO GO

HATTA (123 E5) (*🕮 L 5*)
This oasis at the foot of the Hajar Mountains, 115km (71 mi) east of Dubai, is the traditional summer residence of the locals. Around halfway there you will reach the 100-m (328-ft) sand dune Al-Hamar, also known as the ● *Big Red*, a piece of desert right out of an oriental picture book. Unfortunately you will have to share this dune with lots of other people, in particular young locals racing through the sand on four-by-fours and quad bikes. It is quieter to be out and about on a camel and there are plenty of companies offering that too.

Hatta (population: 10,000), surrounded by mountains, has an excellent *Heritage Village* and a historical fort with two newly erected towers. *Sat–Thu 8am–8pm, Fri 2.30am–8pm | Entry 3Dh*

Hatta Fort Hotel *(50 rooms | tel. 04 8 52 32 11 | www.hattaforthotel.com | Moderate)* is a fascinating option on account of its superb location, in a tropically designed park with views of the Hajar Mountains. In addition, there are organized trips to the Hatta Pools, gorges and pools carved out of the granite rockface over thousands of years; water now flows all year round and swimming is possible.

The term 'oasis' really fits the bill at the Hatta Fort Hotel

SHARJAH

MAP INSIDE BACK COVER

The third-largest emirate (2600sq km / 1000sq mi) is special because of its location, for its beaches lie on two seas, on the Arabian Gulf and the Gulf of Oman in the Indian Ocean.

The second tourist centre after the city of Sharjah is the enclave *Khor Fakkan* on the east coast. With its sandy beach at the foot of the Hajar Mountains (up to nearly 1500m / 5000 ft), it is a paradise for diving and snorkelling. The enclave of *Kalba* (along with Khor Kalba) as well as parts of *Dibba* on the southern east coast are also part of Sharjah (population: 950,000). As in the other emirates, a large proportion of Sharjah's population (75 percent) are from other countries, mainly India and Pakistan. The emirate possesses significant oil and gas reserves and also has highly productive industrial facilities. In addition, it is considered the service centre of the UAE.

Sharjah was the first of the emirates to open up to international tourism, in around 1970. When alcohol was banned in 1985 the influx of visitors shifted to up-and-coming Dubai. For the past few years the emirate has been at pains to attract tourists again: the main target groups are families and those with an interest in culture. Sharjah remains conservative when it comes to Islamic values; alcohol is still taboo and a 'decency law' makes it an offence to dress in beachwear or cropped tops in public.

Photo: Roundabout in sharjah city

Culture and tradition on the sea: magnificent buildings in the Islamic style and a wealth of museums are the pride and joy of the emirate

CITY **WHERE TO START?**
Get a taxi to drop you off at the **Museum of Islamic Civilization** on Corniche Road. Stroll westwards along Corniche Road for a little bit until you get to the Arts Area; on the other side of Al-Boorj Avenue (this is where you will find Al-Hisn Fort) is the Heritage Area with the Al-Arsah Souk and many other historic buildings.

SHARJAH (CITY)

(122 C4) (∭ J 3) **The car-free streets in Sharjah's city centre are lined by whitewashed townhouses and palaces, their ornamental window lattices and massive wooden doors their only ornamentation. Electrified oil lamps provide illumination after dark.**

The city of Sharjah possesses the most

beautiful old town in the UAE. The main reasons for this is that very few of its houses were pulled down after the dis-

in Sharjah are adorned with Arab-style elements.

Take a taxi to the car-free old town, a

Arabian architectural elements adorn the Central Souk (Blue Souk) in the old town

covery of oil and many old buildings were extensively renovated a few years ago. Another reason is that on the initiative of the emir, Sheikh Sultan bin Moham-med al-Qasimi, a large museum quarter has been built in the old town.

Along the 1km (0.5km) *Al-Qasba canal*, which connects Khalid Lagoon with Al Khan Lagoon, you will find French bistros and Italian restaurants, and a musical fountain that shoots water into the sky. Nonetheless the Arabian setting is revealed not just by the locals, who are shrouded in traditional clothing, but also by the palatial buildings, which incorporate Islamic architectural features. At the behest of the emir, all public buildings

unique collection of historic merchant houses and palaces. The two neighbouring quarters, the Heritage Area and the Arts Area, are among the most interesting quarters of the emirates. Sharjah's two dozen museums focusing on Islamic tradition and the region's history or promoting contemporary artistic activities on the Arabian Gulf led Unesco to proclaim Sharjah the Cultural Capital of the Arab World in 1998. The city has also been chosen by the Organization of Islamic Conference to be the Capital of Islamic Culture 2014. The campus of two large universities (American University of Sharjah and University of Sharjah) cover more than 6sq km (2sq mi).

Other neighbourhoods in the city also have plenty of low-level houses from the pre-oil era that are gradually being restored; they are interspersed with skyscrapers.

In contrast to Dubai, the city of Sharjah possesses mainly mid-range hotels, which are located along Khalid Lagoon and the sea. The citizens (approx. 800,000), who appreciate the cheaper rents and good educational facilities, are willing to put up with the ever-lengthening tailbacks, especially to and from Dubai, that living in Sharjah entails. The main group commuting to Dubai, 10km (6mi) to the south, are *expatriates* from the lower income groups. Unbelievably, the morning drive along Sheikh Zayed Road can take up to two hours, as can the return journey in the evening.

SIGHTSEEING

AL-HISN (SHARJAH FORT)

The historic fort of the emir's family (1820) was pulled down in 1969 and re-built true to the original in 1997. It houses exhibitions about the history of the emirate. *Sat–Thu 8am–2pm | Al-Boorj Avenue*

ARCHAEOLOGICAL MUSEUM ★

This is an exciting journey back in time even for those who do not usually enjoy museums. Exhibits from excavation sites, films, interactive computer games and realistic replicas of millennia-old houses and tombs bring the ancient history of Sharjah to life. Museum visitors will learn how the first settlers built their houses, what they ate, the kind jewellery that they made and wore, and how they dealt with death.

The oldest archaeological discoveries date back to the Stone Age (5000–3000 BC), and there are ivory combs and gold and jade necklaces dating from the Bronze Age (up to 1300 BC) on display. *Mon–Thu, Sat 9am–1pm and 5pm–8pm, Fri 5pm–8pm | Cultural Square | Sheikh Rashid Bin Saqr al-Qasimi Road | Al-Abar*

★ Archaeological Museum
Impressive exhibits, perfectly and elaborately presented → p. 63

★ Arts Area
Museums, studios, galleries: the whole world of Arabian art → p. 64

★ Museum of Islamic Civilization
A treasure trove of Islamic culture in a magnificent building → p. 65

★ Sharjah Aquarium
Sharks, sea horses and clown fish are some of the creatures in this colourful marine world. View them up close from the underwater tunnel → p. 66

★ Qanat al-Qasba
Sharjah's rendezvous has smart bistros, restaurants and cafés on the canal → p. 66

★ Central Souk (Blue Souk)
This extravagantly designed building contains more than 600 shops. Explore the large antique market on the first floor, a tempting place to spend money → p. 68

★ Sharjah Desert Park
Get to know the landscape and animals of the Arabian Peninsula in the company of gazelles and desert foxes → p. 71

MARCO POLO HIGHLIGHTS

ARTS AREA ⭐

The Arts Area is home to many restored 19th-century buildings, some of which house museums, including a modern art museum (an extension of Sharjah's Art Museum), with works from the 18th century (*Sharjah Museum of Contemporary Arab Art*). The `INSIDER TIP` Obaid al-Shamsi building on Arts Square, opposite the *Art Museum (Sat–Thu 9am–1pm and 5pm–8pm)*, houses studios, workshops and galleries around a courtyard; you can watch artists at work here. The *Arts Café* on Arts Square is a characterful stop-off for snacks, fruit juices and coffee on your stroll through this attractive quarter. *Shuwaihyeen | between Al-Boorj Avenue (east side) and Corniche Road | www.sharjahart.ae*

BAIT AL-NAHBOODAH

This traditional home of a pearl dealer, dating from 1845, consists of 16 rooms surrounding a courtyard on two floors. The run-down house made of coral stone was restored on the emir's orders and transformed into a museum. The rooms are adorned with lots of stucco work and wood carvings. You can see items of traditional clothing and jewellery, antique furniture and lots of handicrafts. The house presents an impression of what life was like in the Emirates before the oil boom. *Sat–Thu 8am–8pm, Fri 4pm–8pm | entry 5Dh | free guided tours | Heritage Area | Fireij Al-Souk Road, opposite Souk al-Arsah | www.sharjahmuseums.ae*

BUHAIRAH CORNICHE

The waterfront promenade that runs along Khalid Lagoon is lined by palm trees, with flowers adding a splash of colour, and a newly built mosque dominating the view. An old dhow has been transformed into a restaurant, and there's a traditional coffee house. If you want to take a boat ride on the lagoon there are plenty of small boats waiting for passengers. *Buhairah Corniche*

GREEN BELT PARK

There is a 14ha (34 acre) park at Cultural Square that is only open to women and girls, and boys up to the age of eight. Surrounded by a dense, high hedge, this tranquil, green oasis has playgrounds and sporting facilities as well as a small lake with fountains, water jets, flower gardens and an open-air stage. It has four entrances (one on each side). *Sun–Thu 2pm–6pm, Fri / Sat 8am–6pm (ladies only) | free admission | To the northeast of the Cultural Square, south of Green Belt Road (Street 115)*

MAHATTA MUSEUM

Sharjah's airport was located within the city until 1977, and what is now King Abdul Aziz Street was the runway. An old hangar next to the old tower has been converted into a museum housing four propeller planes, one of which hangs

LOW BUDGET

▶ Sharjah possesses more than 20 excellent museums. It costs 5Dh to visit each one, but you can get a ticket allowing access to all them for just 15Dh, which is valid for a month.

▶ The *Book Mall* is the best bookshop in Sharjah, and it also has an inexpensive café for snacks and internet access. *Sat–Thu 9am–10pm, Fri from 4pm | Al-Khan Road | Al-Majaz, near Al-Qasba Canal, between Khaled Lagoon and Al-Khan Lagoon | tel. 06 5 74 45 55*

from the ceiling. The planes, including a Dakota DC3, flew in and out of this airport from 1932 onwards. A film informs visitors about aviation in the 1930s. *Sat–Thu*

MUSEUM OF ISLAMIC CIVILIZATION ★

Sharjah's best museum, which is also the only one of its kind on the Arabian Peninsula, is housed in the former Souk

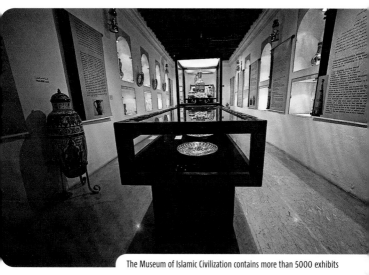

The Museum of Islamic Civilization contains more than 5000 exhibits

8am–8pm, Fri 4pm–8pm | King Abdul Aziz Street, corner of Istiqal Street | Qasimiya

MAJLIS AL-MIDFA

This building possesses the **INSIDER TIP** only round wind tower in the Emirates that is decorated by blue ceramics. One of the restored buildings of the Heritage Area, it is currently closed. *Heritage Area | between Souk al-Arsah and Corniche Road*

MARITIME MUSEUM

This large high-tech museum, which opened in 2009, celebrates Sharjah's seafaring history. It has displays of traditional boats (models and full-size) as well as equipment used for pearl diving. *Sat–Thu 8am–8pm, Fri 4pm–8pm | Al-Mina Road | Al-Khan*

al-Majarrah. Visible from quite a distance, the building, constructed in the Islamic style in 1987, is of brown stone, with striking ornamental lamps, arched walkways and domes. The golden dome is decorated with mosaics on the inside. The museum has some 5000 exhibits, which are superbly presented and give an outstanding insight into the complex belief system of Islam. The ground floor is dedicated to an illustration of the five pillars of Islam. Among the highlights on display are valuable editions of the Koran and – a special treasure for every Muslim visitor – a piece of the *kiswah*, the brocade cloth embroidered with gold that covers the Kaaba in Mecca (Saudi Arabia) and is replaced each year. On the first floor, four galleries take visitors on a journey from the sources of Islamic artistic endeavour to the modern era. *Sat–Thu 8am–8pm, Fri 4pm–8pm | Majarrah Waterfront | Souk al-Majarrah | www.islamicmuseum.ae*

OLD CARS CLUB & MUSEUM

Here are some 100 vintage cars, including a 1917 Dodge with wooden wheels that was a gift from the King of Saudi Arabia. Among the other exhibits, all of them owned by the Emir, are a flawless 1973 Rolls Royce, a 1959 Buick Saloon and a Mercedes Benz 600. *Sat–Thu 8am–2pm, 4.30pm–9pm, Fri 4.30pm–9pm | entry 5Dh | Al-Dhaid Road (next to the airport)*

QANAT AL-QASBA ★

This is where Sharjah shows off its smart, cosmopolitan side: boutiques and European-style cafés and restaurants are housed in new, palatial buildings. It comes to life during the late afternoon. A canal 1km (0.5 miles) long and around 30m (100ft) wide was built from Khalid Lagoon to Al-Khan Lagoon, on which small *abras* (tourist boats) sail back and forth. Three pedestrian bridges cross the water. The ☼ ● 'Eye of the Emirates' also stands on the canal. It has 42 air-conditioned capsules that take passengers up to 60m (200ft) into the air for views over Sharjah and even Dubai *(www.qaq.ae)*.

SHARJAH AQUARIUM ★ ●

Built in an attractive location on the lagoon, Sharjah's high-tech aquarium has some 250 different species of marine inhabitants from the Arabian Gulf, from exquisite seahorses to menacing-looking sharks. There is an impressive tunnel through which visitors can walk and view the underwater life all around. The ☼ cafeteria with views of the lagoon is very popular. *Mon–Thu 8am–8pm, Fri 4pm–9pm, Sat 8am–9pm, Wed only families | entry 20Dh | Al-Khan Road | Al-Khan Lagoon | www.sharjahaquarium.ae*

SHARJAH ART MUSEUM

This two-storey museum, flanked by two wind towers, is the pride and joy of Sharjah's Art Area. Pictures from the Emir's collection and contemporary art by artists from the Arab world are exhibited in 68 rooms. There are changing exhibitions every year, and it is also the venue for the Sharjah International Art Biennale, an event of international standing; the next one will be held in May 2013. In addition to sculptures and installations, provocative video productions regularly create a stir, such as one on the controversial subject of Dubailand, a proposed entertainment extravaganza that was halted by the global recession. *Sat–Thu 8am–8pm, Fri 4pm–8pm | free entry | Bait al-Serkal, Arts Area | Shuwaihyeen, between Al-Boorj Avenue (east side) and Corniche Road*

INSIDER TIP ▶ SHARJAH CALLIGRAPHY MUSEUM

Even though calligraphy in the form of Koranic verses is widely seen in the Emirates, this museum is currently the only one in the Arab world, apart from Tareq Rajab Museum in Kuwait, that is dedicated to this artistic tradition. Even a brief stroll through the museum is worth it to see the exquisite examples of calligraphy on display. For visitors with more than a passing interest, staff are on hand to explain the art and the significance of individual manuscripts. *Sat–Thu 8am–8pm, Fri 4pm–8pm | Heritage Area | between Al-Boorj Avenue (west side) and Corniche Road*

UNIVERSITY CITY

The large and impressive campus, with its pretty gardens, is situated to the east of the city and is home to two universities and several colleges and academies. Take a walk through the area to view the magnificent neo-Islamic architecture, and stop off at its cafés and restaurants for a small insight into what student life is like in the Emirates today. *Al-Dhaid Road, opposite the airport | Al-Mowaileh*

FOOD & DRINK

INSIDER TIP ► **AL-ARSAH COFFEE SHOP**

This is the epitome of what we imagine an Arabian coffee house to be like, with decorated wooden benches, oriental cakes and pastries, Arabian coffee and peppermint tea. Hookahs are available with various tobacco flavours. *Daily | Souk al-Arsah, Heritage Area | between Al-Boorj Avenue (west side) and Corniche Road | Budget*

GERARD

The smell of freshly baked croissants always attracts plenty of customers. This French-style café offers a selection of European pastries, baguettes and walnut bread (also available to go), as well as coffee specialities. *Daily | Qanat al-Qasba, Block A | tel. 06 5 56 04 28 | Moderate*

SARAVANA BHAVAN

Eat in the company of Indian guest-workers at this restaurant specialising in southern Indian cuisine, with exclusively vegetarian dishes. *Daily | King Faisal Road | Abdul Aziz Building | tel. 06 5 73 57 31 | Budget*

SHABABEEK

Lebanese cuisine with European elements is served in a top-class location on Qasba Canal. You may have problems deciding where to sit: outside by the water or in the dramatically designed and opulent Arabic interior. Try the delicious lemonade and mocktails, non-alcoholic

The only thing not served at Café and Bistro Gerard is alcohol

cocktails. *Daily | Qanat al-Qasba, block B | tel. 06 5 54 04 44 | Expensive*

jewellery and perfume shops that cater to local tastes, while the first floor re-

The Souk al-Arsah has 60 small shops, all wonderfully restored

SHARJAH DHOW RESTAURANT

Al-Boom, a traditional Arab trading vessel, was transformed into a floating restaurant. In addition to the standard Arab specialities *(hummus, kebab)*, it also serves a selection of Chinese food *(prawn curries, chicken fried rice)* as well as fish and grilled dishes. *Daily | Khalid Lagoon | Buhairah Corniche, next to the Holiday International | tel. 06 5 73 02 22 | Moderate*

SHOPPING

CENTRAL SOUK (BLUE SOUK, SOUK AL-MARKAZI) ★

This souk, which is notable for its extravagant design, possesses more than 600 shops. The basement has mostly clothing,

sembles INSIDERTIP a large antique fair. The souk is a treasure trove for interior decorators, who come here to seek out unusual furniture, antiques and decorative objects in the oriental and Asian styles. The prices are moderate and are also negotiable, so don't be afraid to haggle. *Daily 10am–1.30pm and 4pm–10pm | Buhairah Corniche Road | Khalid Lagoon | Al-Majaz*

INSIDERTIP SOUK AL-ARSAH

This old souk has been completely refurbished, yet it maintains its special character, as the 60 small shops have been renovated using reclaimed construction materials, such as old wooden beams and doors. Stroll through its narrow streets and discover a bookshop with a large selection of English-language literature about the UAE and books about Islam, as well as high quality antiques from Oman and Yemen, traditional Bedouin clothes and embroidered pashminas. You can take a break from all this browsing by visiting a traditional coffee house. *Sat–Thu 9am–1pm and 4pm–9pm, Fri from 4pm | Heritage Area, between Al-Boorj Avenue (west side), Al-Ayubi Road and Corniche Road*

BEACHES

Do not underestimate the power of the sea off Al-Khan or Al-Mina Street and the hotel beaches here. Occasional currents have been known to drag swimmers out to sea. The beach in front of Sharjah Corniche Road is safer, although it also tends to be crowded.

SPORTS & ACTIVITIES

JAZIRIA (JAZEERA) PARK
A turning off the road from Sharjah to Dubai to the island of Jazirah in Khalid Lagoon leads to a large amusement park and a small petting zoo, including a fun fair, pools and a miniature railway. *Sat–Thu 3.30pm–10.30pm, Fri 9.30am–10.30pm | entry 5Dh | Jazirah Island*

SHARJAH NATIONAL PARK
This national park, measuring more than 60ha (150 acres), is the largest of Sharjah's 35 parks, and features a 'Sharjah Miniature City', with models of the shopping malls and attractions, a four-lane giant slide, a traditional coffee house, a small zoo and a bicycle rental shop – a rarity in the UAE. Be aware, however, that you are only allowed to use these bicycles within the park. *Sun–Thu 4pm–10pm, Fri / Sat 10am–10pm | free entry | Al-Dhaid Road | intersection 5 (3km after Airport Bridge)*

SHARJAH LADIES CLUB
This includes a large ice rink for women and children (boys up to the age of 10), which is a good place to meet the locals. *Sat–Thu 9am–6pm | 35Dh per hour incl. the ice skates | Al-Corniche Road | Al-Seef (road to Ajman, near Al-Muntazah Square) | tel. 06 5 06 77 77 | www.slc.ae*

ENTERTAINMENT

Since alcohol is not available in Sharjah, nightlife has shifted to neighbouring Dubai. To compensate for this Sharjah is at pains to promote its cultural life, with poetry readings, exhibitions and music evenings taking place all year round. *Information from the Sharjah Tourism Authority.* Every week culinary theme nights, such as an Italian night and an Arabian night, take place in the hotels, sometimes with musical performances. Otherwise the only ones awake in Sharjah after 11pm are the nocturnal animals of the Sharjah Desert Park.

WHERE TO STAY

AL-BUSTAN BEACH HOTEL
This inexpensive, older hotel possesses some rooms with sea views, and also has suites and family rooms. Facilities include a popular fish restaurant, a rooftop pool, an internet café and a gym. It also offers shuttle transport to Dubai and free airport transfers, but has no guest parking. *110 rooms | Al-Khan Road | Al-Khan | tel. 06 5 28 54 44 | www.albustangroup. com | Moderate*

AL-SHARQ
A mid-range establishment with small but comfortable rooms, Al-Sharq has a health club, Al-Basha-Restaurant with views of Rolla Park, and shuttle transport to the beach and shopping centres. *63*

rooms | Al-Arooba Street | Rolla Square Garden | Centre | tel. 06 5 62 00 00 | www. sharqhotel.com | Budget

BEACH HOTEL

This older-style beach hotel has rooms with balconies and sea views, though the interiors are a little antiquated. It has a wide, well-tended beach, the largest pool in town and a free shuttle to Sharjah city centre and to Dubai, as well as basic restaurants and cafés. *131 rooms | Al-Mina Road | Al-Khan | tel. 06 5 28 13 11 | www.beachhotel-sharjah.com |* Moderate

CORAL BEACH HOTEL

This hotel is situated at the (northern) border with Ajman. Its interior is luxurious and clean, and it is set amidst palm trees and tropical plants. There is a romantic pool complex and several good-quality restaurants and cafés; plus tennis courts and a gym. There is a Kids' Club in the winter months. *156 rooms | Al-Muntazar Road | tel. 06 5 22 99 99 | www.coral-beachresortsharjah.com |* Expensive

HOLIDAY INTERNATIONAL

This high-rise hotel on Khalid Lagoon has a quiet, attractive setting. It offers a shuttle to Dubai, two pools, tennis courts and a gym, and has several restaurants and cafés, including the excellent fish restaurant Fishermen's Wharf, offering views of the pool and the lagoon. *253 rooms | Buhairah Corniche | tel. 06 5 73 66 66 | www.holidayinternational.com |* Moderate

MARBELLA RESORT

At the 4-star hotel tailored to families, guests can choose between villas and suites. The buildings are constructed in the Arab-Andalusian style and are surrounded by lush gardens. The rooms' interiors are somewhat staid, but the leisure activities on offer (tennis, two pools, squash, gym) are excellent and the restaurants are among the most popular in the city. It also has a rather grand marina and runs shuttle to Dubai. *100 suites and villas | Khalid Lagoon | tel. 06 5 74 11 11 | www.marbellaresort.com |* Expensive

PLAZA

Offers small, basic rooms (sometimes loud) in the city centre, plus a restaurant and coffee house. *57 rooms | Al-Qasimi Road | Government House Square, Municipality R/A | Al-Gharb | tel. 06 5 61 70 00 | plazahotel@emirates.net.ae |* Budget

MANGROVE SWAMPS

The ☺ nature reserve *Khor Kalba* is also part of Sharjah. It is an enclave of the emirate on the east coast, to the south of Fujairah city, on the border with Oman. It is one of only a few mangrove swamps still extant in Arabia. It consists of low-growing trees and shrubs, which are able to flourish in seawater, thereby creating a unique ecosystem. The reserve is home to rare waterbirds, fish and lots of different micro-organisms. Mangrove swamps, with their typical dense stilt roots, are declining all around the world, threatened by oil and other pollution as well as by commercial fish farming. Take a rental car across a bridge to the south of Kalba to get to the Khor Kalba Nature Reserve.

Holiday International has a view of Khalid Lagoon

SHARJAH YOUTH HOSTEL

On the road to Ajman, it offers dorms (3–5 beds each) with balconies, a communal kitchen and laundry facilities. *40 beds | Bait Shabab | Al-Merkab Street 262 | Shargan (near Muroor R/A) | tel. 06 5 22 50 70 | www.uaeyha.com | Budget*

INFORMATION

SHARJAH COMMERCE & TOURISM DEVELOPMENT AUTHORITY

Buhairah Corniche | Crescent Tower, 9th Floor | Al-Majaz (near Al-Qasba canal) | tel. 06 5 56 67 77 | www.sharjahtourism.ae

WHERE TO GO

SHARJAH DESERT PARK ★
(127 D4) (*K 4*)

The extensive Desert Park, with its outstanding *Natural History Museum,* possesses one of the Emirates' best zoos. It began with an initiative by the ruler to protect the oryx, which is at risk of extinction. Photographs and documents provide information about the flora and fauna on the Arabian Peninsula, and there are displays of shell collections, unusual fossils and large crystals found in the desert.

One section, the *Botanical Museum,* is dedicated to desert plants, while *Arabia's Wildlife Centre* is home to approx. 100 animal species, including nocturnal desert dwellers. In addition to the *Aquarium* there is also a *petting zoo (Children's Farm),* where children can get close to and feed the semi-tame mammals in an outdoor enclosure. Sitting in the café, you can watch antelopes, ostriches and giraffes in a savannah-type landscape behind glass. *Wed–Sun 9am–7pm, Fri 2pm–7pm | entry 15Dh | on the road from Sharjah to Al-Dhaid: Sharjah – Al-Dhaid Road | Intersection 9 | 25km (15 mi) east of Sharjah city*

AJMAN &
UMM AL-QAIWAIN

Ajman and Umm al-Qawain, the two emirates to the north of Sharjah city and Dubai, don't possess oil and are financially supported by the federation. The locals you'll meet here work as fishermen and farmers, preserving an impression of what life used to be like on the gulf.

The tiny emirate of *Ajman* (population: 290,000), just 260sq km (100sq mi) and framed by Sharjah, possesses a 16-km (10mi) coastline, at the northern end of which Ajman city is located. Tourism centres on the beautiful sandy beach, where only a few hotels have been built to date. If you're after a quiet holiday by the sea, especially one that is far cheaper than in Dubai or Abu Dhabi, then Ajman is the right choice. The two enclaves of

Masfut, 110km (68mi) to the southeast, which has a mineral water spring, and *Manama,* 60km (37 mi) to the east near Al-Dhaid, agricultural settlements that supply produce for all of the emirates, are also part of Ajman.

A large bay, protected from the open sea by several islands, is the natural landmark of *Umm al-Qawain*. The emirate, which lies to the north of Sharjah, has an area of 777sq km (300sq mi) and hardly more than 95,000 inhabitants, by and large cordial down-to-earth Emiratis who live off fishing, farming and trade. Ten islands in the bay, some of which are covered in mangrove swamps, are home to rare breeding birds, while giant turtles and sea cows swim around in the sea. The 40-km (25mi) coastline is unde-

Photo: Umm al-Qaiwain, Old Fort

Two small emirates – the clocks tick slower here than in their bigger neighbours

veloped, with very few beach hotels. The oasis of *Falaj al-Mu'alla* (50km/30mi) southeast of the capital) is very fertile; thanks to plentiful stores of groundwater the land here is farmed intensively.

AJMAN

(122 C3) (*⌀ J 3*) **Lively but untouched by the glamour and building boom of the richer emirates, the city of Ajman (population: 270,000) makes up al-** **most the entire emirate. It has older, low-level concrete buildings and has a mix of Arabian and Indian influences.**

A typical scene in Ajman would be of men sitting together over a glass of tea or a mango juice in one of the simple tea houses, while veiled women, their hands adorned with striking henna tattoos, assess the goods in the shops – typical Emirati clothes, scented oils and Far Eastern electronic goods. Since Ajman is home to many *expatriates*, particularly from India, for whom Dubai and Sharjah are too expensive to live, there are also many outstanding Indian restaurants. Ajman's beach is sandy and golden but not ideal for swimming because of its strong currents.

few traditional dhows are anchored, is also located in this bay. These are all good place to experience what life was like in the UAE before the building boom. *Khor Ajman*

Caribbean ambience on the private beach of the luxurious Ajman Kempinski hotel

SIGHTSEEING

AJMAN MUSEUM ★

For around 200 years this fort-like building housed the emirate's ruling family. Two guard towers flank the entrance gate, outside which a replica souk depicts what daily life was like before the oil boom. The fort houses exhibits on Islamic tradition, handicrafts and displays about Bedouin medicine. *Sat–Thu 9am–1pm and 4pm–7pm | entry 5Dh | Aziz Street, at Al-Hosn R/A*

AJMAN SOUK

All that's left of the former souk in the northeast of the city, in a small bay of Ajman Creek, is the *Vegetable Market* and the *Fish Souk* as well as the *Iranian Souk* selling household items. The *Fishing Boat Harbour*, in which fishing boats and a

FOOD & DRINK

BUKHARA

Here the spicy northern Indian cuisine is prepared in a lighter style, popular among Europeans. *Daily | Sheikh Humaid Bin Rashid al-Nuaimi Street (Ajman Corniche) | Kempinski Hotel | tel. 06 714 55 55 | Expensive*

FALCON

Serves good falafel sandwiches, kebabs and *ful medames.* Locals and migrant workers from Pakistan meet here for dinner on weekends, when it also has a buffet. *Daily | Al-Khaleej Road (Ajman Corniche) | Ajman Marina Club | tel. 06 742 33 44 | Moderate*

WHERE TO STAY

AJMAN BEACH HOTEL

This hotel, nicely situated between palm trees on the waterfront, has rooms with views of the sea or the creek. Has watersports, beach volleyball, bars, a nightclub and a restaurant (Arabian cuisine) and offers a free shuttle to Dubai. *68 rooms | Ajman Corniche | tel. 06 7 42 33 33 | www. ajmanbeachhotel.com | Budget–Moderate*

AJMAN KEMPINSKI ⚜

Offering luxury accommodation in the opulent Arabian style, Ajman Kempinski is surrounded by palm trees and right on the sandy beach. The rooms are smart with fantastic sea views and a balcony. Amenities include a fitness and health club, watersports, a large pool, a diving school and a spa with INSIDER TIP ayurveda treatments. *182 rooms | Sheikh Humaid Bin Rashid al-Nuaimi Street (Ajman Corniche) | tel. 06 7 14 55 55 | www. kempinski-ajman.com | Expensive*

INFORMATION

Information is available from the museum.

UMM AL-QAWAIN

(123 D3) (Ø J3) The capital of the emirate (population: 55,000), often shortened to UAQ, lies at the northern end of an elongated peninsula. The old town runs around a small bay to the west of the creek, in which dhows and fishing boats are anchored.

Umm al-Qaiwain has not yet been reached by the construction and restoration wave that has swept through the

---

CITY WHERE TO START?
Drive along the peninsula's east side on Sheikh Ahmed Bin Rashid al-Mualla Road and head northwards, past the market and Palma Beach Hotel, then past a park and to the **harbour basin**. Park there and then continue on foot around the harbour to the Al-Qaiwain Museum in the fort. From here, take a stroll through the old town and the west side to Park Corniche Garden,

larger emirates, and few of its men, who dress in the traditional white *dishdasha*, possess expensive cars or real estate. Most live a simple life, and like to chat with friends in the cafés, playing board games and smoking the hookah. Umm al-Qaiwain lies 25km (15mi) to the north of Sharjah and can be reached from there by car or taxi in half an hour.

SIGHTSEEING

INSIDER TIP **OLD TOWN**

Between newer buildings, housing small shops, there are quite a few older houses made of coral stone in the Arabian style, but unfortunately they are threatened

---

MARCO POLO HIGHLIGHTS

★ **Ajman Museum**
The ancient fort of the ruling family is now a museum
→ p. 74

★ **Umm al-Qaiwain Museum**
The historical treasures of the emirate are on display in the old fort → p. 76

by decay. The most important treasures are the three guard towers, once part of the old town wall *(soor)*, which are now being restored. They can be found to the west of the old town along Al-Soor Street. *Between Al-Soor Street and Mualla Road*

UMM AL-QAIWAIN MUSEUM ★

Surrounded by high clay walls and dominated by round towers, the former fort (1770) of the rulers of Umm al-Qaiwain is now being restored as a museum. The individual departments present the *majlis* (the traditional meeting room of the na-

1st–2nd-century containers in the Umm al-Qaiwain Museum

tive men), an archaeological collection of discoveries from the region, as well as a traditional kitchen. *Sun–Thu 8am–1pm and 5pm–8pm, Fri 5pm–8pm | entry 5Dh | Al-Lubna Road | Old Town*

VEGETABLE AND FISH MARKET

Every morning lively haggling takes place at the small vegetable and fish market. It is best to come early in the mornings when the fishermen bring in their catch from the night before. *Sat–Thu 7am–1pm and 4pm–8pm | Sheikh Ahmed Bin Rashid al-Mualla Road | eastern side of the town, north of Pearl Hotel*

FOOD & DRINK

AQUARIUS

Basic but tasty and inexpensive Asian food is served at this restaurant on the beach. Fish dishes are the speciality. *Daily | Sharjah-RAK Road | Barracuda Beach Hotel, in front of Dreamland Aquapark | tel. 06 7 68 15 55 | www.barracuda.ae | Budget*

LEBANESE RESTAURANT

Known for its outstanding Lebanese cuisine, including classics like tabouleh salad and falafel sandwiches, and delicious juices. *Daily | UAQ Corniche | UAQ Beach Hotel | tel. 06 7 66 66 47 | www. uaqbeachhotel.com | Moderate*

PALMA

This Arabian restaurant in the hotel of the same name on UAQ Creek is known for its brunch buffet on Fridays. European *expatriates* on weekend getaways and local families meet here during the late morning to enjoy many delicious treats, such as Arabian mezze, cheese or Japanese sushi, hot and cold main courses as well as oriental desserts, in a peaceful setting. *Daily | Sheikh Ahmed al-Mualla Road | Palma Beach Resort | Alhamra Area | tel. 06 7 66 70 90 | Moderate–Expensive*

SPORTS & ACTIVITIES

UAQ MARINE CLUB

The club offers waterskiing *(30 mins, 50Dh)*, windsurfing *(1 hr, 35Dh)* and kayaks for trips into the lagoon. *Daily 8am–7pm | Sheikh Ahmed Bin Rashid al-Mualla Road (next to Pearl Hotel) | tel. 06 7 66 66 44 | www.uaqmarineclub.com*

WHERE TO STAY

FLAMINGO BEACH RESORT

This beach hotel at the tip of the peninsula on the creek has bars and restaurants, a pool and watersports. It also rents boats for trips across the creek and to the island of *Al-Sinniyah* (bird-watching). *52 rooms | Creek Corniche Road/ King Faisal Road | UAQ Tourist Centre | tel. 06 7 65 00 00 | www.flamingoresort.ae | Moderate*

PALMA BEACH RESORT

A pyramid, columns with ancient Egyptian hieroglyphs and portraits of pharaohs are some of the unusual design elements at this beach hotel on the town's east coast. It offers three pools, an internet café and an extensive leisure programme (including bowling, pool and sailing trips). INSIDER TIP Dinner cruises can be enjoyed on the hotel's own dhow. Also bookable if you're not a guest *(tickets in the hotel)*, an entertaining way to spend the evening, though the food is only average. *63 rooms | Sheikh Ahmed Bin Rashid al-Mualla Road | Alhamra Area | tel. 06 7 66 70 90 | www.palma group.ae | Expensive*

UAQ BEACH HOTEL

This quiet beach hotel is great for families. There is no entertainment programme, nor *oriental singers*, but it has a large pool, watersports and a shuttle to Dubai three times per week. *32 suites | UAQ Corniche | tel. 06 7 66 66 47 | www. uaqbeachhotel.com | Budget–Moderate*

INFORMATION

The *Flamingo Beach Resort* acts as the UAQ Tourist Centre *(Creek Corniche Road/ King Faisal Road | tel. 06 7 65 00 00).*

WHERE TO GO

INSIDER TIP **AL-LABSA CAMEL RACE TRACK** (123 D–E3) (*ɰ K3*)

On the road from Umm al-Qaiwain to (and just outside) Falaj al-Mu'alla (45km/28mi) is a camel racetrack. It lies to the north of the road in the wind shadow of high sand dunes. During winter the animals are trained every morning. The camel races are a noisy event, mainly for the enjoyment of local men and migrant workers. Tourists are received with curious stares but are always welcomed. *Camel races Oct–March Thu and Fri from 7am | free admission | E55 Al-Labsa*

LOW BUDGET

▶ There are no public buses in Ajman and UAQ and even taxis are thinner on the ground than in Sharjah. You can get a very inexpensive group taxi to UAQ and Sharjah *(10–15Dh per person)* from the corner of Sheikh Rashid Bin Humaid Road and Al-Karama Street (Ajman centre).

▶ You can enjoy authentic southern Indian cuisine in *India House*, which is even cheaper than the food court. Try the delicious thali: 10 different types of curry and rice. *Daily 8am–midnight | Choitram Supermarket Bldg. | Sheikh Rashid Bin Humaid Road | Al Karama | Ajman | tel. 06 7 44 24 97 | www. indiahouseajman.com*

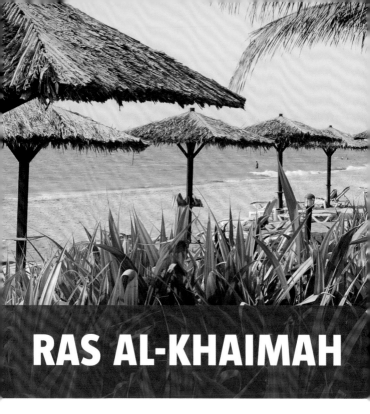

RAS AL-KHAIMAH

With dramatic mountains reaching 1800m (5900ft), large expanses of desert with high sand dunes, long beaches, and villages in green oases, Ras al-Khaimah is the most beautiful of the emirates.

The northernmost emirate, Ras al-Khaimah has a size of 1700sq km (656sq mi) and a population of 250,000. Its mountainous Musandam Peninsula borders Oman and the Strait of Hormuz. It has only a small quantity of oil, but plenty of mountain springs permit a flourishing agricultural sector. It is the breadbasket of the UAE, and supplies the remaining emirates with vegetables, fruit, milk and other dairy products, especially the plains, the area south of the capital and the oasis of Digdagga, 18km (11mi) away.

The 40km (25mi) strip along Ras al-Khaimah's west coast was an important pirate base from the 17th to the 19th centuries. Even today the inhabitants of this emirate are jokingly referred to as 'pirates' by other Emiratis. The proportion of the population that's native is on a par with that in Umm al-Qawain, namely around half, much higher than the more wealthy emirates.

There are several ambitious tourism projects currently under construction. One development, *Al-Marjan Island*, comprises four connected islands that extend 2.5km (1.5mi) into the sea 25km (15mi) southwest of Ras al-Khaimah city (near Al-Hamra hotel). Ten luxury hotels, one marina and several mansions are to be built here. Tennis legend Boris Becker has invested in

Photo: Beach of Al-Hamra Fort

Natural resources and ambitious tourist projects – this emirate is worth visiting

a hotel and tennis academy, which is why he is a regular visitor in the emirate.

Another project is the *Jebel Jais Mountain Resort* and the *Desert Snow Village*, a ski centre complete with pistes and artificial snow on the west side of the Hajar Mountains. The *Mina al-Arab* (Arab Harbour) is a 3-km (2mi) development along the coast to the south of the city, with artificially raised land on which hotels, private homes, lagoons, marinas and parks are being built *(www.minaalarab.net)*.

RAS AL-KHAIMAH (CITY)

(123 E2) *(Ⓜ K2)* **The new town of Ras al-Khaimah is lively and chaotic, the old part is a little more sedate.**

The city of Ras al-Khaimah (population 160,000), 100km (62mi) north of Dubai, is divided by the Al-Khor Lagoon into the western Old Town and the eastern new town of Al-Nakheel, from where Oman Road heads inland. The fort in the Old Town, along with a town wall and cannon, once protected the city, but it is now a national museum. The covered fish market is busy every day, packed with men shopping for their families.

The city's appeal lies in its vibrant juxtaposition of modern shopping malls, office buildings and new construction projects, plus its unspoiled oriental lifestyle. The cityscape is dominated by low,

SIGHTSEEING

INSIDER TIP ▶ AL-FALAYAH FORT

The summer residence of the ruling family from the 18th century, Al-Falayah Fort is surrounded by date-palm groves. It is where the first peace treaty with the British was signed in 1820. Two old towers guard the complex, which also includes one of the oldest mosques in the country. Though not currently open to visitors, the department of tourism plans to create a museum in the tower and a heritage

The National Museum occupies an old fort – wind tower to the right

older buildings, with lots of greenery in between. Close to the centre are wide beaches with fine white sand, while the foothills of the Hajar Mountains are within 10km (6mi) of the city, creating a beautiful panorama. Several luxury real estate projects have already been completed and 5-star hotels attract European investors and visitors. The fact that change is afoot here is felt quite strongly and the number of Westerners you'll encounter here is growing.

park in the courtyard. *Fenced and not accessible | Sheikh Saqr Bin Muhammad al-Qasimi Road | 3km to the southeast, on the road to Digdagga*

DHOW BUILDING YARD

You'll still see several wooden dhows on the beach of Maarid. These are manufactured by hand in the traditional manner by Indian and Pakistani carpenters. Visitors are welcome. *Maarid Corniche | northern end of town*

WHERE TO START?
By car it's best to go to the city centre or the RAK Museum; park outside the **Fort Museum**, then stroll to the corniche on the Arabian Gulf or in the opposite direction to the corniche on the lagoon. You could also take a ferry across the lagoon's canal to visit the Museum & Centre of the Navigator Ahmed Bin Majid.

INSIDER TIP MUSEUM & CENTRE OF THE NAVIGATOR AHMED BIN MAJID

Tucked away in the new town and largely unknown, this museum is dedicated to the famous 15th-century Arab seafarer and cartographer. Boats, naval maps and navigation instruments are on display. *Sat–Thu 4pm–7pm | free admission | Mamourah Road (near the Hilton)*

NATIONAL MUSEUM ★ ●

The emirate's most significant museum is housed in the Old Fort, an impressive building with battlements, guard towers and a small tropical garden. Built between 1736 and 1749 by the Persians and destroyed by the British in 1819, the Old Fort was rebuilt and expanded and became the home, until 1960, of the ruling emir Al-Qasimi and his extensive family. The guard towers and the wind towers are also open to the public, and there is a collection of silver coins from the 10th and 11th centuries on display. The natural history section exhibits a shell and fossil collection as well as tools from the 1st millennium BC. Pottery from Al-Ubaid, Mesopotamia (modern-day Iraq), traded 5000 years ago, as well as exhibits from the Bronze Age tombs of Shimal are among the museum's greatest treasures. Further discoveries were excavated in

Julfar, 3km (2mi) to the north of Ras al-Khaimah, and the Emirates' most significant port between the 14th and 17th centuries. Most of these discoveries are porcelain objects that originally came from China and Iran (the excavation site lies in an industrial estate and is not open to the public). *Sat–Mon, Wed, Thu 10am–5pm | entry 5Dh | Al-Hosn Road | Old Fort*

SHIMAL (SHAMAL)

The archaeological site of Shimal is worth visiting because of a massive and dramatic mountain ridge that towers above the village. It is crowned by the ruins of a formerly fortified settlement, known by the locals as 'Sheba's Palace'. The archaeological discoveries (pottery, now in the museum of Ras al-Khaimah) confirm a surprisingly recent age of 500 years, however. The remains of a well and a cistern can still be seen, but most impressive is the view from the ☆ top, which is fantastic. You can see all the way to Ras al-Khaimah. Archaeologists created a stir in the 1980s, when they discovered 4500-year-old Bronze Age tombs, including an oval tomb with several chambers. The tombs are closed off and can't be visited, but the grave goods that were discovered can be seen in the National Museum in Ras al-Khaimah. *Oman Road | 7km (4mi) to the northeast*

★ **National Museum**
Exhibits range from Bronze Age finds to porcelain from China → p. 81

★ **Al-Dhayah Fort**
The century-old military base has great views from the top of the hill → p. 84

MARCO POLO HIGHLIGHTS

FOOD & DRINK

AL-KHOR
Begin with a cocktail on the terrace, then *hummus* and salad as a starter, followed by steak and seafood. The restaurant, which has views of the pool of the Hilton and the lagoon of Ras al-Khaimah, offers a mix of Arabic and international dishes. *Daily 8am–11pm | Al-Jazah Road | tel. 07 2 28 88 88 | Expensive*

AL-SAHARI
Provides good and inexpensive Arabian food and friendly service. Try baked 'Sultan Ibrahim Fish', the oriental salad and the flat bread. *Daily | Sheikh Mohammed Bin Salem Road | Old RAK (at the post office) | tel. 07 2 33 39 66 | Moderate*

LEBANESE HOUSE
This small restaurant serves good Lebanese cuisine. The mutton and crab kebabs are excellent. *Daily | Muntasir Road (next to the Nakheel Hotel) | tel. 07 2 28 99 92 | Budget*

INSIDER TIP VENUS DELUXE
Offers southern Indian vegetarian cuisine, as well as northern Indian and Chinese specialities. *Daily | Nakheel Road (Al-Rams Road), opposite the Diyafa Residence at the Safeer Supermarket | Al-Nakheel | tel. 07 2 21 21 64 | Moderate*

SHOPPING

MANAR MALL
The largest shopping mall in Ras al-Khaimah, Manar Mall is home to 110 shops (including several international names), a large Carrefour supermarket, self-service restaurants and cafés. *Daily | Al-Nakheel Road | www.manarmall.com*

SOUKS
Souks for textiles, gold, fish, and fruit and veg can be found in the Old Town.

SPORTS & ACTIVITIES

INSIDER TIP CAMELRACE COURSE
You can watch the camels being trained on the 10km (6mi) circular course on Friday and Saturday mornings. Races take place on the same days, from 2pm (Apr–Oct). *Al-Sawan | Digdagga | 9km (5mi) to the southeast*

Manar Mall is the largest shopping centre in Ras al-Khaimah

RAK WATER SKI CLUB
A slalom course has been set up in the shallow water of the lagoon, with options for both beginners and experienced waterskiers. *Sat–Thu 10am–5pm | 60Dh (6 x Slalom) | Corniche Road | Khouzam (southern shore of the lagoon behind the RAK-Hotel) | tel. 07 2 36 44 44*

SAILING TRIP
The fjord landscape of Musandam can be explored on board the motorised Monalisa. The boat has two-master and six double cabins and sails from Ras al-Khaimah via Khasab, Kumzar and Lima through the Strait of Hormuz to Dibba. Stops at fishing villages and beaches interrupt the sailing trip, which is frequently accompanied by dolphins and whale sharks. *Arabia Horizons Tours| 807 Golden Business Center| Airport Road| Dubai | tel. 04 2 94 60 60 | www.arabia horizons.com| overnight $589 incl. meals*

WHERE TO STAY

AL-HAMRA FORT
This luxurious and large beach hotel is situated 18km (11mi) south of Ras al-Khaimah city. It has pools, a fitness suite,

tennis courts, a children's club and watersports. *155 rooms | Al-Jazeerah Road | tel. 07 2 44 66 66 | www.alhamrafort.com | Expensive*

AL-NAKHEEL
Seven-storey basic hotel in the new town, with a lively pub and an Arabian restaurant. *55 rooms | Muntasir Road | Al-Nakheel | tel. 07 2 28 28 22 | Budget*

BANYAN TREE AL WADI
This exclusive hotel runs a unique nature reserve for gazelles and other animals needing protection and teaches its guests about the environment. Guests are put up in Arabian-inspired villas with a pool. The smart designer bathrooms, which feature large windows from which you can survey the landscape, are like works of art in themselves. There's hardly a nicer place in which to experience the desert in its natural state and to fall in love with the magic of Arabia. Upon request you'll be taken to the hotel's own beach club, which is just a few minutes' drive away. *101 Pool Villas | Wadi Al Khadiya (20km/12mi south of RAK city), E311 northbound, Exit 119, then 7km/4mi to the south) | tel. 07 2 06 77 77 | www.banyantree.com | Expensive*

BIN MAJID BEACH RESORT
Offers terraced bungalows with a small terrace and sea views, three pools, 2km (1mi) beach, watersports, beach volleyball, fitness, shuttle to Dubai and RAK. *92 rooms | Al-Jazira al-Hamra | south of Al-Hamra Fort Hotel | tel. 07 2 44 66 44 | www.binmajid.com | Moderate*

JULPHAR
The five-storey building (including rooms with balconies) has a bar and a nightclub as well as an Indian ayurveda centre. Provides free airport transfers (Sharjah

and Dubai). *39 rooms | Al-Jazah Road | Al-Nakheel (opposite the Expo Centre) | tel. 07 2 28 88 84 | www.julphar-hotel. ae | Budget*

Al-Dhayah Fort, weathered by time

KHATT SPRINGS HOTEL & SPA

Visible from afar, this hotel towers atop a hill in the style of an Arabian fort and is located next to Khatt Springs. Two of its own pools are fed by the mineral spring. The hotel attracts guests with its luxurious rooms, a modern spa and a fitness suite. Other leisure facilities are quite limited, however. INSIDER TIP Entry to the public baths is free to guests of the hotel *(otherwise 25Dh)*. Operates a free

daily bus shuttle to Ras al-Khaimah city, the mall and to Al-Hamra Fort Beach Resort. *150 rooms | Khatt Springs | 20km to the south | tel. 07 2 44 87 77 | www.khatt hotel.com | Moderate*

RAK HOTEL

Comfortable hotel with large rooms, some with sea views, plus two pools, sauna, tennis, squash, a restaurant serving international cuisine, and the Garden Room Coffee shop serving Lebanese cuisine. *100 rooms | Eid Khouzam Road | tel. 07 2 36 29 99 | www.rakhotel.net | Moderate*

INFORMATION

RAK TOURISM OFFICE
P.O. Box 31291 | Al-Jazirah Al-Hamra | Ras al-Khaimah | tel. 07 2 44 51 25 | www.rak tourism.com | www.rakpedia.com

WHERE TO GO

AL-DHAYAH FORT ★ ☆
(123 E2) (*∅ K2*)

The fort, which was partially restored in 2001, was built in the 18th century on the ruins of a clay-brick Portuguese fort built during the 16th century and subsequently extended. It has two towers and stands on top of a hill (there is a concrete staircase at the back), from where there are extensive views of the date palms of Dhayah, the Hajar Mountains and the Arabian Gulf. In 1819 the fort was seized by the British and severely damaged. *Daily 8am–noon and 3pm–6pm | free entry | Rams Road | 13km/8mi to the north (northeast of Rams)*

INSIDER TIP AL-JAZIRAH AL-HAMRA
(123 D2) (*∅ K3*)

This abandoned fishing village right on the water *(around 20km/12mi to the south)*, once stood on a reddish sandbank that became an island during high tide, hence the name 'red island' (*jazirah* = island, *hamra* = red). Today the surrounding area has been filled in artificially and is part of the mainland. The inhabitants have moved to new homes further inland, but maintain a small fishing harbour to the north of the village. Few of the people still live in the ruins. The derelict houses are dominated by the mosque's intact minaret. Walk around the village to get give an understanding of how people built and lived in days gone by, without oil or wealth. Old guard towers rise up between the ruins.

KHATT SPRINGS (123 E3) (*ᗰ K3*)
The village of Khatt, 20km (12mi) to the south of Ras al-Khaimah city, is worth an excursion. A mineral spring (40°C / 104°F) supplies two pools in a public bath (separate for men and women) as well as a hotel's wellness area. The sulphurous water is reputed to help skin and rheumatic problems, and is popular with locals. *Daily 8am–10pm | entry 25Dh*

SHAMS (123 E1) (*ᗰ L2*)
Head along the west coast towards the Omani province of Musandam. After 30km (19mi), just before the border, you'll come across the fishing village of Shams, which is partially built into the mountainside. Some of the houses almost disappear into the rock. The settlement has held on to its original character, and visitors should be discreet.

WADI BIH ☖ (123 E–F2) (*ᗰ L2*)
The Hajar Mountains runs from Musandam in Oman for 600km (370mi) in a southeasterly direction through the UAE and Oman, reaching altitudes of 1800m (5900ft) in Ras al-Khaimah. A good way of exploring this mountain range is via a tour into the *Wadi Bih*. Towering rocks in all shades of brown and grey, steep hairpin tracks, with fantastic views, the wadi runs eastwards from Ras al-Khaimah city through the mountains to Zighy Bay on the east coast. The complete trip has to be done in a four-by-four, because only some of the journey is surfaced. Since you'll pass through UAE border controls and the border to Oman, you'll need to take your passport but no other formalities are required.

Start at sunrise at the southern end of town at Lantern R/A on Oman Road and head eastwards. After 5km (3mi) you'll pass Coffeepot R/A and begin ascending into the foothills. The road turns into a track and then climbs in hairpin bends, and the wadi gets narrower. Before returning to the coast, take a break on the wonderfully empty plateau. In the deserted, silent landscape and clear light you may spot faraway objects such as goatherds.

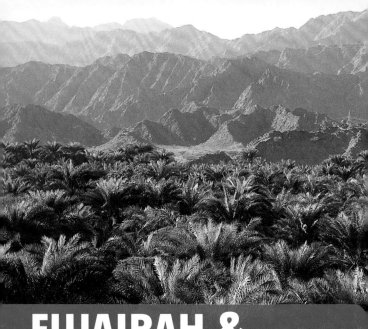

FUJAIRAH & THE EAST COAST

With sandy beaches and deep-blue water, palm trees, and the peaks of the Hajar Mountains on the horizon, the scenic east coast is one of the most beautiful parts of the Emirates. Bordering the Gulf of Oman are the emirate of Fujairah (population: 130,000) as well as a few enclaves of Sharjah. The region developed for centuries in isolation from the other emirates, not least because the colder and deeper waters prevented pearl diving from flourishing. Oil wasn't found on the east coast. However, the strategic location on the Gulf of Oman prompted the richer emirates to build two harbours as well as a road across the Hajar Mountains. That way, during political conflicts or problems in the Strait of Hormuz, important import

goods could still be brought into the country safely and then distributed. This strategic advantage gave the east coast a certain affluence.

The east coast is suffering increasingly from polluted beaches and other environmental problems, and for that reason a seaside holiday here isn't always a fully positive experience. The beaches are polluted by oil and tar residue from time to time, since tankers on the way to the ports of Fujairah and Khor Fakkan as well as to the Strait of Hormuz presumably clean their tanks in the waters here. Seaweed and jellyfish populations have also increased in recent years.

The fertile valleys of Fujairah and its 50 villages and date-palm groves are ruled by Sheikh Hamad bin Mohammed Al

Photo: Hajar Mountains

Green landscapes and bull fighting, dramatic mountains and fertile valleys characterise this small emirate on the Indian Ocean

Sharqi. The people farm poultry and, thanks to a reservoir, are able to achieve high agricultural yields. For some years now Fujairah has tried hard to promote tourism. Visitors with a passion for diving are particularly attracted to the area, since the underwater world of the Gulf of Oman, with its coral banks and rocky sea floor, has more to offer than the flat and sandy west coast.

South of Fujairah city and belonging to Sharjah are Kalba and the lagoon of *Khor Kalba*, a unique natural landscape covered in (now rare) mangrove swamps and home to many species of bird.

Sharjah's exclave of *Khor Fakkan* (population: 40,000) lies at the geographical centre of the east coast. It is home to the Oceanic Hotel built in the 1970s and, because of its round roof terrace restaurant, a long-established landmark in the region. Several 3–5-star hotels have been built along the beaches south of Dibba, in the north of Fujairah.

Fujairah Fort appears to have grown straight out of the rocks

FUJAIRAH (CITY)

(123 F4) (*M L4*) The capital of Fujairah (population: 70,000) lies in the southern part of the east coast. At first glance it is not a very attractive town. It is dominated by a container harbour, has a refinery on the outskirts, and has a lot of traffic.

It wasn't until the 1980s that Fujairah city got its first hotel and a (hardly used)

> **CITY WHERE TO START?**
> When approaching from Khor Fakkan, drive along Al-Faseel Road all the way to Coffeepot R/A, then turn right into Al-Nakheel Road; the **Fujairah Museum** lies on the right-hand side beyond the next roundabout. Park your car there and stroll through the ruins of the Old Town, with its clay houses, to the historical Fujairah Fort.

international airport. The beach is not very inviting, so most visitors drive the scenically stunning coastal route, which in places has views of the Hajar Mountains. It is around 150 km (93 mi) from Dubai to Fujairah city.

SIGHTSEEING

INSIDER TIP BAIT SHEIKH SAEED BIN HAMAD AL-QASIMI
The mansion of the ruling family of Sharjah has been turned into an ethnographic museum. The palatial building, with its many rooms, now houses a collection of traditional costumes, antique household objects, as well as tools and a coin collection. *Kalba Fort (Al-Hisn)* opposite the museum is currently closed to the public and it's not certain when it will reopen. *Sat–Thu 9am–1pm and 3pm–8pm | entry 3Dh | Kalba Corniche | Al-Hisn area*

FUJAIRAH FORT ★ ●
Located on a small rocky hill in the middle of the run-down Old Town is the historic fort, which dates from 1670. The

structure was extended several times, and now consists of three main buildings and several guard towers. The fort, surrounded by clay ruins, is said to be the oldest in the Emirates; it was seriously damaged by the British in the early 20th century. From the viewpoint you can see the restored clay brick constructions of the walls and towers. *Sat–Thu 9am–1pm, Fri 2pm–6pm | entry 2Dh | Al-Salam Road, corner Al-Kalla Road | Old Fujairah*

FUJAIRAH MUSEUM

The modern museum near the fort exhibits discoveries from the Fujairah, including bronze coins, in its archaeological section and old tools and Bedouin jewellery in the ethnographical section. *Sat–Thu 8.30am–1.30pm and 4.30pm–6.30pm, Fri 2.30pm–6.30pm | entry 5Dh | Al-Gurfa Street, corner Al-Nakheel Road*

HERITAGE VILLAGE

Here, barasti huts and old fishing boats take you back to Fujairah's past. Old household objects, tools and agricultural equipment reveal what life was typically like in Fujairah just a few decades ago. A well illustrates how water was obtained prior to desalinating the seawater. *Sat–Thu 9am–1pm and 4pm–7pm, Fri 3pm–7pm | free entry | northern end of Al-Ittihad Road*

FOOD & DRINK

AL-MESHWAR

The stone cladding of this house is fake, but the Arabian specialities are delicious. The café on the ground floor serves snacks, while Lebanese cuisine can be enjoyed on the first floor. *Daily 9am–midnight | Hamad Bin Abdullah Road | tel. 09 2 23 11 13 | Moderate*

INSIDER TIP ROYAL CAFETERIA

This is a simple waterside café serving Arabian snacks, situated on the road to Kalba. It serves delicious hummus and falafels and crisp *oriental salads* for next to no money. Drink sweetened hot tea from plastic beakers, while greeting migrant workers from India and Pakistan and gazing out at the ocean. It doesn't have to be expensive to be good! *Daily | Corniche Road South | tel. 09 2 22 66 88 | Budget*

THAINESE

The name says it all. Thainese serves Chinese and Thai food, with the added bonus of good sea views. *closed Sat | Corniche | International Marine Club, 1st Floor | tel. 09 2 22 09 69 | Moderate*

SPORTS & ACTIVITIES

AIN AL-MADHAB

The 50ha (120 acre) park attracts many local visitors with its lush vegetation and

---

★ **Fujairah Fort**
The historical fort towers above the derelict walls of the Old Town → p. 88

★ **Bidyah Mosque**
At the foot of the Hajar Mountains, this is the Emirates' oldest mosque → p. 91

★ **Bithnah Fort**
This date palm oasis is dominated by an impressive fort → p. 91

★ **Khor Kalba**
Nature reserve with flamingos, cormorants and more besides → p. 92

MARCO POLO HIGHLIGHTS

a sulphurous mineral spring. There are several pools, a restaurant and a café, as well as various barbecue spots and basic bungalows for spending the day here. *Daily 9am–10pm | entry 3Dh, Bungalow 100Dh, use of the pool 5Dh | northern end of Al-Ittihad Road*

INSIDER TIP ▸ BULL BUTTING

This is bull-fighting Arabian style. The fenced-in, sandy bullring comes to life on a Friday afternoon, when massive zebu bulls are brought to the venue on the back of a pick-up truck. Swaying into the arena via a wooden ramp, they are a sight to behold. Two well-matched bulls are brought face to face, and then the *mattah*, 'head-butting', begins, and little more than that. Even committed animal lovers are reasonably happy with this relatively gentle variety of bull fighting. *Fri afternoons | free entry | Bullring | southeastern end of town between Fujairah Corniche and Al-Muhait Road*

LOW BUDGET

▶ There are two *youth hostels* on the east coast: in Khor Fakkan *(24 beds | Corniche Road | next to Al-Khaleej Club | tel. 09 2 37 08 86)* and Fujairah city *(48 beds | 203 Al-Fazil Area | tel. 09 2 22 23 47)*. The accommodation is inexpensive (75Dh). *www.uaeyha.com*

▶ A day at the sulphurous spring of *Ain al-Madhab* is good for your health and only costs 3Dh to enter, and 5Dh to use the pool. *Daily 9am–10pm | northern end of Al-Ittihad Road | Fujairah*

WHERE TO STAY

INSIDER TIP ▸ BREEZE MOTEL

This is a small hotel on the water, 12km (7mi) south of Fujairah. It has a restaurant on a beach with the same name. Family rooms are available, and miniature golf and a pool are among the amenities. It is inexpensive and has a great location. *34 rooms | Kalba Corniche Road | tel. 09 2 77 71 13 | www.breeze motel.com | Budget*

FUJAIRAH YOUTH HOSTEL

Accommodation in two-storey four-bed dorms, with a dining room, communal bathroom and small kitchen. *48 beds | Bait Shabab | Al-Fazil Road | tel. 09 2 22 23 47 | www.uaeyha.com | Budget*

HILTON FUJAIRAH

This hotel lies on a well-tended private beach between palm trees. It has modern rooms, plenty of facilities and a relaxed atmosphere in the restaurants and bars. The *Sailor's Restaurant (moderate)* on the beach is well worth seeking out for its outstanding fish and seafood. *92 rooms | Al-Faseel Road | tel. 09 2 22 24 11 | www.hilton.de/fujairah | Expensive*

MIRAMAR AL-AQAH BEACH RESORT

Built in the Moroccan style, this three-storey holiday complex for families has 200m (218 yds) of private beach, pools (including an indoor pool), tennis, beach volleyball, kids' club, wellness & health club and a fitness suite. The villas, in the colours of the desert, are set in front of a magnificent mountain landscape; inside, archways and chandeliers give them an oriental atmosphere. *321 rooms | Al-Aqah | 15km (9mi) south of Dibba, 45km (28mi) north of Fujairah city | tel. 09 2 44 99 94 | www.iberotel.de | Moderate*

Fujairah Observer *(monthly, free, www. fujairahobserver.ae)*

FURAIRAH TOURISM BUREAU
Hamad Bin Abdullah Road | Trade Centre | tel. 09 2 23 15 54 | www.fujairah-tourism. gov.ae

WHERE TO GO

BIDYAH MOSQUE ★ (123 F3) (*ω L3*)

There is an art-historical gem on the road north of Fujairah city, with fantastic views over the rocks, sea and palm trees. The small white, unadorned complex, dominated by two old guard towers, stands out from the grey rocks; its four domes and unusual central column are made out of clay. Thought to date from 1466, it is believed to be the oldest mosque in the Emirates. It is open to the public. *Usually 9am–noon | free entry | Khorfakkan–Dibba Road | Al-Bidyah | 35 km north of Fujairah (city)*

BITHNAH FORT ★ (123 F4) (*ω L4*)

If you take the road from Fujairah towards Masafi, you'll pass a beautiful oasis with a small fort, built in 1745, surrounded by palm trees. Behind the town are extensive date-palm groves, intersected by old walls and several wadis. Just outside town a viewpoint offers good views of the fort, which was built in a strategic location to guard the Wadi Ham on the old route through the Hajar Mountains from Fujairah to Sharjah. The partially derelict fort is currently being restored and can only be viewed externally. *28km (17mi) to the west of Fujairah ciy)*

DIBBA (123 F3) (*ω L3*)

A fishing village (population: 10,000), on the northern border to the Omani province of Musandam, Dibba is divided into three areas: *Dibba Muhallab*, which belongs to Fujairah, *Dibba Hisn (Sharjah)* and Omani *Dibba Bayah* (there's just a brief passport inspection at the border there). Even though Dibba is a new town with active construction, its large natural harbour, golden sandy beaches and the Hajar Mountains on the horizon all contribute to its attractiveness as a destination. There are several hotels along the beaches:

Simple but beautiful: Bidyah Mosque

The ⚲ *JAL Fujairah Resort & Spa* has large rooms, all of them with a terrace or balcony and panoramic sea views, as well as restaurants, cafés and bars, various pools and a Zen Spa, a renowned Padi diving centre and a chic INSIDER TIP library (books, newspapers, magazines) with internet access. Romantic, cool, with sea views, the hotel's *Moon Beach Lounge* with rooftop access is the place to while away the evening until the early hours of the morning, sipping cocktails and smoking a hookah. *257 rooms | Dibba | tel. 09 2043111 | www.jalfujairahresort.ae | Expensive*

The well-known *Sandy Beach Hotel* also has an outstanding beach location, but the interior is relatively basic. It is also appreciated by divers (it has its own diving base) and is situated opposite tiny *Snoopy Island. It* has rooms with terraces leading onto the beach, as well as chalets with one to three bedrooms and own barbecue spots. *28 chalets and 40 rooms | Al-Aqah | Dibba | tel. 09 2445555 | www.sandybm.com | Budget–Moderate*

Rug vendors show off their wares at Masafi Friday Market

KHOR FAKKAN (123 F3) *(🕮 L3)*

The busy east coast port of Sharjah (population: 40,000) has a splendid corniche that runs from the *Oceanic Hotel* to the town and is frequented by lots of people out for walk at dawn and dusk. The large Ocean Hotel, which is several decades old– it shows – stands out because of its round ☀ roof restaurant. There are good views of the sea and the beach from its windows.

The *Padi diving centre (www.oceanichotel.com)* next door caters to beginners and experienced divers alike with daily diving trips into this area's impressive underwater world.

The Emir's summer palace on the hillside across from the Oceanic Hotel is striking. An old guard tower, dating from the early 16th century, is a reminder of Portuguese rule here (1507–1650). In fact, the Portuguese seafarer Vasco da Gama was the first European to describe Khor Fakkan, in 1498. There are cafés and a restaurant along the beach, which is lined by palm trees, from where you'll also have wonderful panoramic views of the mountains. *25km (15mi) to the north of Fujairah city*

KHOR KALBA ★ (123 F5) *(🕮 L4)*

A wide corniche runs south from Fujairah city to Kalba and Khor Kalba. There are parks and gardens shaded by palm trees, and cafés, restaurants and playgrounds between the road and the beach. The *Breeze Motel (see p.90)* with its beach restaurant *(between Kalba and Khor Kalba)* is a good place to take a break.

The entrance to the ☺ *Khor Kalba* nature reserve is via a bridge. There are picnic sites by the roadside. Arabia's oldest mangrove swamp, which extends for 7km (4mi) in two tidal lagoons, is home to many flamingos, cormorants and other birds. Fishing boats anchor in the lagoon, while the fish cooperative's ice factory can be seen on land. The light just before sunset is exquisite and perfect for taking atmospheric photographs of the lagoon. *12km (7mi) to the south of Fujairah city*

MASAFI FRIDAY MARKET
(123 E4) *(🕮 L 3–4)*

This is more of a photo opportunity than a place to go shopping, but it is original and authentic. Indian and Pakistani traders haggle over exotic fruits, wooden blinds, Pakistani carpets, ceramic goods, plants, inflatable plastic toys and a lot more to the left and right of the road to Al-Dhaid. *Daily 8am–9pm | Al-Dhaid Road | Masafi | 35km (22mi) from Fujairah city*

MUSANDAM
(123 F 2–3) (L 2–3)

Dive into the wild, inaccessible world of Musandam Peninsula, which is rich in scenic highlights and beautiful landscapes: the northern Omani exclave of Musandam is nicknamed 'the Norway of Arabia', as it possesses remote fjords, dominated by high mountains and small, isolated villages, unaffected by the modern world. The waters are crystal-clear and are ideal for snorkelling, diving and swimming. INSIDER TIP Boat trips in traditional dhows to the Omani fjords are run from Dibba *(Arabia Horizons | Golden Business Centre | Airport Road, next to Honda | Dubai | tel. 04 2 94 60 60 | www.arabiahorizons.com | overnight $589 incl. meals with hotel pick-up in Dubai, Shar-jah, RAK and Fujairah | You will need to bring a passport with a visa for the UAE or Oman).*

The most beautiful and luxurious hotel on the east coast is the ● INSIDER TIP *Six Senses Hideaway Zighy Bay*. The resort is right on the sea and looks like a rustic fishing village, and the emphasis here is on nature and natural products. The accommodation comprises stone villas with a pool, outside showers and a 24-hour butler service. The spa is tempting, and the views over dinner from the observation deck of the 'wind tower' are enchanting. Since this hotel is in Oman, you will have to show your passport at the checkpoint along the road when arriving by car, but you won't need a visa. *79 Pool Villas | Zighy Bay | 20km (12mi) north of Dibba: 12km (7mi) of surfaced road – 5km (3mi) dirt road to the reception – 4km (2mi) in the hotel's own jeep | tel. 00968 26 73 55 55 | www.sixsenses.com | Expensive*

Refreshing tranquillity in a wild environment: snorkelling in Musandam

TRIPS & TOURS

The tours are marked in green in the road atlas,
pull-out map and on the back cover

① FROM SHARJAH TO THE INDIAN OCEAN

The day trip to the Emirates' east coast starts in Sharjah, goes past Sharjah Airport and continues on the E88 via Al-Dhaid to Masafi, then through the Hajar Mountains, either via the northern route to Dibba or via the southern route to Fujairah city, then along the east coast and subsequently back to Sharjah. There and back is roughly a 300-km (180mi) trip. Hotels and travel agencies offer an equivalent bus tour. If you're travelling in a rental car it's worth spending a night in one of the northern beach hotels or in Fujairah city.

It's 55km (34mi) from Sharjah to Al-Dhaid, a large trading place for agricultural products with several workshops and Indian and Pakistani restaurants at the side of the road. It's not worth spending any time here and there are quite a few roundabouts to contend with while driving through the town.

Drive on for another 33km (20mi) to Masafi at the foot of the Hajar Mountains; the elongated village is home to a huge street market → p. 93. Masafi means 'pure water' and that's also the name of the major mineral water bottler on the road to Dibba. The village belongs to the emirates of Ras al-Khaimah and Sharjah and there are mango trees as well as lime and orange trees in the vicinity, as well as springs around the edge of the mountains. After crossing

Travel through dramatic mountain ranges and fertile valleys, experience the vastness of the desert and take in fascinating mangrove swamps

the mountains on the northern route through gorges and green valleys, you'll reach the town of Dibba → p. 91 on the Gulf of Oman. If you're travelling by hired car, you could add in an excursion to Oman 20km (12mi) away (just a quick passport check on the road) and stay in the Six Senses Hotel 'Zighy Bay', which has a lovely spa. The approach is truly breathtaking: hotel guests park their cars at the entrance to the resort and are then taken steeply uphill in an off-road vehicle, up into the barren mountains. At

the top, there are fantastic views of the sea and the hotel in its solitary location at the foot of the mountains.

If you drive south from here, after a few kilometres you will see the small mosque of Bidyah → p. 91 at the foot of the mountains, guarded by two old towers. As it is a historic monument, it is free to visit. Next you will reach Khor Fakkan → p. 92; the well-known Oceanic Hotel is located at the northern end of town and can be identified by the round structure on the top of it. A waterfront promenade runs from there to the centre. After 20km (12mi) you will reach Fujairah city → p. 88, whose old town and fort are worth visiting. To the south of the city is the seaside town of Kalba and the adjoining nature reserve Khor Kalba → p. 92, a lagoon with mangroves. The return journey goes via Fujairah city and Bithnah → p. 91 and its fort to Sharjah.

Those who aren't really that enamoured with Fujairah – and you have to look for its attractive spots as they are not on the main road – should continue along the sea towards Kalba. When navigating roundabouts, always take the road leading towards the sea. Fort Kalba, 10km (6mi) to the south of Kalba, on the right-hand side, can only be photographed from the outside. Beyond the fort there are fruit and vegetable markets as well as a fish market on the corniche. After 12km (7mi) you will reach Khor Kalba, a suburb of Kalba; pass the Breeze Motel, then, 2km (1mi) further on, cross the bridge that leads into Khor Kalba nature reserve, a lagoon with mangrove swamps.

17km (11mi) south of Fujairah, there is a sign to a tunnel that runs through the mountains, leading to a road to Sharjah.

2 FROM DUBAI TO ABU DHABI AND AL-AIN

Take a rental car on the E11 along the coast of the Arabian Gulf to Abu Dhabi (165km/100m), then take the E22 highway, which is lined by tropical vegetation, to Al Ain (160km/10mi) and finally cross the desert on the E66 back to Dubai (135km/84mi). With a night in Abu Dhabi and another in Al Ain, this is a three-day tour. Buses (Emirates Express) run on all three of these routes several times a day, so that this tour can also be done by bus.

Leave Dubai → p. 50 southbound on the E11 and drive to Jebel Ali in heavy traffic between lorries and past several building sites; it's only afterwards that you'll cross the large area of flat salt desert that runs along the coast of the Arabian Gulf.

From Jazirah Hotel (halfway) it's another 42km (26mi) to the turning on to the E10 to Abu-Dhabi city → p. 33, which is then another 30km (18mi) away.

When travelling by rental car, you will get a good impression of the rapidly changing city and Abu Dhabi's island location. Large signs indicate in good time that the highway turns into three multi-lane bridges, which lead to Abu Dhabi city. If you take the central one, Maqta Bridge, which crosses the narrow Khor al-Maqta canal, you will see Al Maqta tower standing in the shallow water. It is one of the last remnants and reminders of a time when camel caravans approached the city and stayed the night in the caravanserais to the left and right of the tower, which are all gone now. Bear right after crossing the bridge and drive northbound along the eastern side of the island of the city to get on to the Eastern Corniche, from where you will have good views of the long mangrove islands and extensive green spaces along the corniche. Driving to Yas Island, which lies just outside the city, is also worthwhile. A huge leisure resort with dozens of luxury hotels is being built here. Yas Hotel, which opened in 2009, is spectacular. It is a futuristic building between the new marina and the Formula 1 racetrack.

If you are going to spend a day here, visit Corniche Park by the sea, the Emirates-Palace hotel and the Sheikh Zayed Grand Mosque. If you are going to spend the night here, good sightseeing options for

One of several restored forts houses the Al Ain Palace Museum

the next morning are the Heritage Village and the Old Fort (White Fort).

Abu Dhabi's highway to Al-Ain is lined by oleanders and date palm, beyond which are vegetable fields and forestation projects. Al-Ain → p. 44, the birthplace of the state founder Sheikh Zayed, which has grown from being a traditional oasis into a modern town, has diverse activities on offer to visitors: several restored forts, a national museum, the best zoo in the Emirates and an genuine camel market. If you choose to stay a further day, it is worth visiting the Omani town of Buraimi → p. 49 (visa required) and do the 12km (7mi) drive up 60 hairpin bends to the top of 1,348-m (4,423ft) Jebel Hafeet. This three-lane road – lit at night – goes up past the Grand Mercure hotel (915m/3,000ft) and palaces of the ruling family to a plateau, from where you'll have lovely views. At the weekends the locals come to the surfaced square, which is flanked by mountains, to enjoy watching the falcons circling the summits. On the way back from Al-Ain to Dubai, visit a 5000-year-old round tomb in Hili Archaeological Park → p. 46.

3 FROM ABU DHABI TO LIWA OASIS

Liwa Oasis → p. 43 is situated around 230km (142mi) to the southwest of Abu Dhabi city and extends in a large arc along the edge of the desert of Rub al-Khali (Empty Quarter) for more than 100km (62m) westwards from Hamim towards Arrada. A round trip (approx. 450km/280mi) can be done in a rental car in one day, as 300km (186mi) are on highways, but it's a good idea to spend the night in the main town of Mezirah.

Drive from **Abu Dhabi city** → p. 33 to the E11 (30km/19mi) and head south to the turning to Hamim (20km/12mi). The E65 country road runs in a dead-straight line across 140km (87mi) of desert. After 20km (20mi) you will see a huge Landrover model to your left, which houses a shop stocking provisions. Here you will find Sheikh Hamad's pyramid-shaped **INSIDER TIP** *National Auto Museum (daily 7am–5pm | entry 50 Dh | www.enam.ae)*. It exhibits more than 200 vintage and unusual cars, including a Mercedes 300 'Adenauer'; a cafeteria – between a large globe, exotic caravans and a water tower – serves fresh juices.

After Hamim the four-lane road winds its way westwards through dunes and plantations, past farms and lots of villages, before reaching **Mezirah,** the main town of Liwa Oasis, after 50km (30mi). This town lies at the geographical centre of the east–west road along which the other towns in the oasis lie. The highlight of a visit to Liwa Oasis is a trip through the desert to **INSIDER TIP** *Moreeb Hill*, a sand dune almost 300m (985ft) high and 1.6km (1mi) long 30km (19mi) south of Mezirah. This is what everyone imagines a desert to look like. Spend a night in **Liwa Hotel** *(61 rooms | Mezirah | tel. 02 8 82 20 00 | www.ncth.com | Moderate)*, a comfortable hotel with a large pool, restaurant and excellent Indian cuisine, and with views of the surrounding desert, or stay in the basic, rustic and romantic **INSIDER TIP** *Liwa Resthouse (21*

Liwa Oasis is almost like a mirage in the desert

rooms | Police Station Road | Mezirah | tel. 02 8 82 20 75 | Budget) on a hill behind the police station on the road to Moreeb Hill. Liwa Oasis is one of the stops of the Abu Dhabi Desert Challenge that takes place in October (www.uaedesertchal lenge.com). It's one of the races in which drivers score points for the FIA Cross Country Rally World Cup.

The return journey will take you north via Medinat Zayed (65km/40mi), a modern town that has little to interest tourists) to the E11 (50km/30mi), then 110km (68mi) northeastwards on the E11 to Abu Dhabi.

4 INSIDER TIP THROUGH THE MANGROVE SWAMPS BY CANOE ☺

The Dubai-based business Desert Rangers offers individual exploration tours through the mangrove swamps of Khor Kalba, the exclave of Sharjah to the south of Fujairah on the border with Oman. One of the options is to travel to the lagoon from Dubai with the Desert Rangers (2 hrs) or to meet them there to pick up the canoes. After a short introduction you'll be allowed to get out on the water.

The landscape is a joy to all lovers of the outdoors. On the horizon behind the lagoon the Hajar Mountains, and the only sounds are of birds singing and the splashing of the water when the paddle strikes it. The water is so clear in some places that crabs and fish and even turtles are visible.

The mangroves themselves are evergreen trees and bushes with thick stilt roots that go down into the saltwater and supply the plants with water and nutrients.

You can glide through the water for two to three hours, and if you're in the mood it's also enjoyable to simply stop in a particularly lovely spot to enjoy the scenery: water, mountains, trees and canoeists in harmony. If you're out and about during the hours of sunset, you'll witness the dramatic changes in the colours of the sky and in the sounds of the birds and animals. When it's time to return to civilization you'll probably find it seems even louder and busier than before. (Desert Rangers, tel. 04 3 57 22 33 | www. desertrangers.com | minimum number of participants: 4 people | 300 Dh per person from Dubai. 150 Dh from Khor Kalba. Other operators also offer tours in the mangrove swamps: e.g. Flamingo Beach Resort in UAQ, Kayak Club Abu Dhabi, Noukhada Abu Dhabi)

SPORTS & ACTIVITIES

The two coastlines have wide beaches and an exotic underwater world, delivering the best conditions for watersports, and many of the hotels offer equipment, tuition and facilities. If you want to join the locals, go sand-boarding in the desert or ice-skating in several of the cities.

BALLOONING

Flights in a hot-air balloon over the desert and dunes of Dubai are run by *Balloon Adventures Dubai (Oct–May | tel. 04 2 85 49 49 | www.ballooning.ae | Dubai)*. Hotel pick-up at around 5am, flight around 1 hour, plan for around 5 hrs. Around 950Dh per person.

DESERT SAFARI & DUNE-SKIING

Trips into the desert, usually with a picnic, camel rides, a bit of folklore and even a little bit of belly dancing, as well as a try at sand-boarding or dune-skiing, are organized by *Net Tours (Abu Baker Siddique Road at the Clock Tower, opposite the Hamarain Centre | Al-Bakhit Centre, 1st Floor, Plot 185, Regga Al-Buteen | Dubai | tel. 04 2 66 66 55 | www.nettoursdubai.com)* and *Khalifa Street (opposite the Sheraton | Abu Dhabi | tel. 02 6 79 46 56 | www.netgroupauh.com)*.

DIVING

Diving is only really worth it on the Emirates' east coast, as the west coast is too

There's plenty to do in the Emirates, from diving and sailing to riding, ballooning, dune-skiing, playing golf and ice-skating

sandy and flat. Dives are offered by the *Sandy Beach Diving Centre* in the *Sandy Beach Hotel*, halfway between Dibba and Khor Fakkan *(Al-Aqqa | Fujairah | tel. 09 2 44 50 50)*. The diving depths are 3–18m (10–60ft) and attractions include Snoopy Island, 100m (330ft) from the hotel, and an artificial reef of 200 car wrecks 1,500m (1,650yds) from the shore. Also on Padi basis (Professional Association of Diving Instructors) with lessons.

FOOTBALL

Football is a popular sport in the UAE, and new stadiums are being built everywhere. Al Ahli Dubai plays in the UAE's professional league (its coaches are from UK and have Premier League experience). Important matches are held in Al Rashid Stadium. The spectators are largely native Emiratis, with only a few Asian migrant workers among them, meaning the stands are usually 'all in white'. The mood is the same as it is everywhere else, namely noisy and excited, but there are no hooligans and nobody gets aggressive. *Matches on Fridays, less commonly during the week, in the late afternoon or early evening | Al-Rashid Stadium | Al-Nahda Road | Al-Nahda 2 | Dubai | entry often free | Metro: GGICO*

GOLF

The Emirates have lots of world-class golf courses, most of them in Dubai.
Abu Dhabi Golf Club | Green fees 325–795 Dh | Sas al-Nakhl | tel. 02 5 58 89 90 | www.adgolfclub.com; Sharjah Golf Club | Green fee 9 holes from 180Dh | Dhaid Road | 3rd Interchange, Paintball Park | tel. 06 65 48 77 77 | www.golfandshootingshj. com. The *Tower Links Golf Club* in Ras al-Khaimah has a website: *www.towerlinks. com.* Several golf clubs in Dubai, including the *Emirates Golf Club* and the *Dubai Creek Golf Club*, can also be booked online: *www.dubaigolf.com*

HORSE RIDING

The *Abu Dhabi Equestrian Club* offers hacks, show jumping sessions and lessons. *Al-Mushrif | between Khalifa Bin Shakbout Street (28th Street) and Karama Street | Entrance next to Mushrif Palace | Abu Dhabi | tel. 02 4 45 55 00 | www.adec-web.com*
Jebel Ali Golf Resort & Spa to the south of Dubai offers one-on-one riding lessons *(70Dh/30 mins)* and accompanied hacks into the desert *(150Dh/hr)*. *Oct–May Tue–Sun 7am–noon and 4pm–7pm | Jebel Ali | Dubai | tel. 04 8 83 60 00 | www.jebelali-international.com*
Sharjah Equestrian Club offers hacks and one-on-one lessons. *Al-Dhaid Road, corner of New Dubai Road, 17km (11mi) outside Sharjah city | Sharjah | tel. 06 5 31 11 55 | www.forsanuae.org.ae*

Playing golf on the lush greens of Jebel Ali Golf Resort

ICE SKATING

Dubai, Abu Dhabi and Al-Ain all have large ice rinks, and sometimes the shopping malls also have one.

Dubai Ice Rink | daily 10am–noon, 12.15pm–2.15pm, 2.30pm–4.30pm | Dubai Mall | Sheikh Zayed Road | 1st Interchange, Doha Street | Dubai | 2 hours 50Dh (incl. skates) | www.dubaiicerink.com

Abu Dhabi Ice Rink | daily 10am–10pm | entry 5 Dh, 2 hours' skating including skates 15 Dh | Zayed Sports City | Airport Road | Abu Dhabi

Al-Ain Ice Rink | daily 10am–8pm | 2hrs 25Dh | Al-Ain Mall, Al-Falaheya Street | Kuwaitat | Al-Ain | www.alainmall.net

LEISURE PARKS

The number of leisure and amusement parks is growing rapidly in Abu Dhabi, Dubai and Sharjah. Information about amusement parks is also available from the hotels and tourist information offices. One large amusement park is *Al-Nasr Leisureland*: it has several sporting facilities such as squash, bowling, go-karting and ice-skating. *Daily 9am–10pm | entry 10Dh | Umm Hurair | Bur Dubai | Dubai | tel. 04 3 37 12 34 | www.alnasrll.com*

SAILING

Sailing boats (also lessons) are kept by the following hotels in Dubai: *Jebel Ali, Hilton, Jumeirah Beach, Meridien, Oasis, Royal Mirage, Dubai Marine*.

SIGHTSEEING FLIGHTS

HELICOPTER

Get an overview of Abu Dhabi in the Eurocopter EC130, run by *Falcon Aviation*. You'll spot Saadiyat and its museums, the Corniche of Abu Dhabi and the spectacular buildings of the Formula 1 island Yas. *10, 20 or 30 mins | 400–1000Dh per person | tel. 02 4 44 00 07 | www.falcon aviation.ae*

SEAPLANES

Another way to sightsee is by seaplane (Cessna 208 Caravan, nine passengers), leaving from Club Joumana in the Jebel Ali Golf Resort and then flying over The Palm Jebel Ali (still under construction), Burj Al Arab, The Palm Jumeirah, home of the Atlantis Hotel and Burj Khalifa, before heading to Dubai Creek. The seaplane lands in Dubai Creek Golf & Yacht Club. Or take the tour to the Emirates Palace in Abu Dhabi, over Ras al-Khaimah and Fujairah. *Seawings Dubai | www.seawings.ae | tel. 04 8 07 07 08 | 40-minute flight 1125Dh, children 955Dh*

WATER PARKS

The Emirates are also keen to break records and garner superlatives for their aquaparks. The *Wild Wadi* and the *Aquaventure* in Dubai both offer vertiginous slides and wild water.

Wild Wadi Water Park | Nov–Aug daily 10am–6pm, Sept–Oct daily 10am–7pm | 205Dh | Jumeirah Beach Road (in front of Burj Al Arab) | www.wildwadi.com

Dreamland Aqua Park | daily 10am–6pm | entry 135Dh | 14km (9mi) north of the UAQ Roundabout on the road to Ras al-Khaimah | Umm al-Qaiwain | www.dreamlanduae.com

WATER-SKIING

The larger beach hotels usually offer water-skiing. *Ras al-Khaimah Water Ski Club* behind the RAK Hotel on the west side of the lagoon Khor Ras al-Khaimah *(Khuzam | tel. 07 3 36 44 44)* is inexpensive.

TRAVEL WITH KIDS

The summer months aren't the best time to opt for a trip to the UAE with children, because it is too hot. During the rest of the year families with children will find plenty to entertain them. The local Arabian population tends to have large families, and the Asian migrant workers like children. This means that they're welcome everywhere.

Every child would like to ride a camel at least once, and there are many opportunities to do so in the UAE, such as in the heritage villages of Abu Dhabi and Dubai, during organised trips into the desert, and often on the beach. Visiting an Arabian fort, with its guard towers and battlements, inspires children and adults alike, as will a stroll through one of the exotic souks.

Lots of the major hotels offer childcare, or even run kids' clubs, and several have special children's pools; discounts for accommodation and buffets are standard. The large shopping malls generally have a play area, and Dubai Mall even has an aquarium *(see p. 55)*.

If you would like to eat in the traditional manner with the locals, restaurants (outside of the hotels) often have a separate *family room*, where Arab women are allowed to take off their veil and eat with their families; foreigners and their children are also welcome guests here.

Photo: Dubai Aquarium

There's plenty of activities and attractions for kids in the Emirates, from camel rides and beaches to aquariums and amusement parks

ABU DHABI

INSIDER TIP AL-AIN ZOO

(127 E–F 1–2) (*⌀ K6*)

The Emirates' most beautiful zoo is worth visiting if only for its stunning design. There's a falconry demonstration in the theatre at 6.30pm, where you can see falcons, owls and vultures, and there are keepers' talks and a giraffe feeding session. *Daily 9am–8pm | Zoo R/A, Zayed Al-Awwal Street/Nahyan Al-Awwal Street | entry 15Dh, children 5Dh | www.awpr.ae*

CULTURAL FOUNDATION (126 B1) (*⌀ G6*)

In addition to exhibiting jewellery, musical instruments and model dhows, the *Cultural Foundation* also runs guided tours for children (in English). The *Children's Centre* has thousands of picture books and children's books. *Closed for refurbishment until autumn 2012. Sun–Wed 8am–10pm, Fri 5pm–8pm, Sat 9am–1pm and 5pm–8pm | Zayed the First (Electra) Street, Ecke Rashid al-Maktoum Road (Airport Road), next to the Old Fort | entry 3Dh | www.adach.ae*

RIDING A BIKE ☺ (130 B1) (*ⁿ G6*)

The 6-km (4mi) Corniche of Abu Dhabi is also INSIDER TIP a park, with special cycle paths in places. Bicycles can be hired in several locations, including next to the Hilton Beach Club at the Breakwater and at the Sheraton end, opposite the Royal Meridien hotel (*20Dh/hr*).

UMM AL-QUWAIN

DREAMLAND AQUA PARK
(123 D3) (*ⁿ K3*)

This aqua park has more than 30 slides, a wave pool, rubber floats and a lot more, and is situated in an extensive park (25ha/60 acres) by the sea, between palms and tropical trees. There is even accommodation here: bungalows cost 235–335Dh per person per night. Sun–

Wild, wet entertainment at Wild Wadi Waterpark

Thu 10am–6pm, Fri / Sat 10am–7pm, Fri / Sat families only | entry 135Dh, children 85Dh | Ras al-Khaimah Road | Umm al-Quwain | tel. 06 7 68 18 88 | www.dream landuae.com

DUBAI

EMIRATES KART CENTRE
(122 B5) (*ⁿ H–J 4*)

An 800m (870yd) go-kart track, with floodlights, for children aged 8 and up; also junior karts for children up to the age of 11. *Daily 3pm–9pm | 20 mins 100Dh | Jebel Ali | next to the Jebel-Ali-Hotel, 40km/25mi south of Dubai | tel. 04 2 82 71 11*

ENCOUNTER ZONE
(122 C4) (*ⁿ J4*)

This hi-tech entertainment centre has various highlights, namely a labyrinth, a haunted room and a 3D cinema, plus craft-making sessions. The *Galactica* is great for teenagers, while *Lunarland* is better for younger children. *Daily 10am–11pm | free entry | Oud Metha Road (from Sheikh Zayed Road) | Wafi City Mall, 3rd floor | www.wafi.com*

KIDZANIA (122 C4) (*ⁿ J4*)

In this replica city, with streets, buildings, shops and cars, 4–15-year-olds can role-play in jobs and 'experience' the world of adults. At the entrance children have to check in as if at an airport. They are issued with a boarding pass (entry ticket), a city map and a voucher for Kidzania money. *Sun–Wed 9am–10pm, Thu 9am–midnight, Fri / Sat 10am–midnight | entry adults from 17 years and up 90Dh, children 4–16 years 125Dh, toddlers 2–3 years 95Dh | Dubai Mall, Financial Centre Road, off Sheikh Zayed Road, 1st Interchange | Metro: Dubai Mall*

WILD WADI WATER PARK ☼
(122 C 4–5) (*J4*)

This aqua park is inspired by the desert and wadi landscapes of the UAE. It has 28 slides and attractions (such as a wave pool and a lagoon where small children can splash around). The Burj Al Arab hotel is opposite and there are sea views. *Nov–Feb daily 10am–6pm, March–May and Sept / Oct 10am–7pm, June–Aug 10am–9pm | entry 205Dh, children 165Dh | between Jumeirah Beach Hotel and Burj Al Arab on Jumeirah Beach Road | www.wildwadi.com*

WONDERLAND (122 C4) (*J4*)

The amusement park for families has more than 30 rides *(Theme Park)* and the *Splashland Waterpark* presents itself as a Disney-inspired theme park, with restaurants, cafés and souvenir shops *(Main Street)*. *Mon–Sat 10am–8pm, Splashland 10am–7pm, Wed women only | entry 75Dh, children 55Dh | Al-Garhoud Road, to the south of Creekside Park at Garhoud Bridge | Bur Dubai | www.wonderlanduae.com*

SHARJAH

DISCOVERY CENTRE (122 C4) (*J3*)

This is a good place for children up to their early teens. The large space has loads of things to discover, and children are playfully inspired to experiment in various different areas and ways, such as sports, the senses, driving, building and the water world. There are play corners for very small children, while schoolchildren are allowed to touch, experiment and play to their heart's content. One particularly popular attraction is a road with small cars, set up to teach children about traffic regulations. The centre is also a chance for young tourists to meet children from Arabia and Asia. *Sat–Tue 9am–2pm, Wed–Fri 3.30pm–8.30pm | entry 10Dh, children 5Dh, families 15Dh | Al-Dhaid Road | Interchange 4, opposite the airport | 15km (9mi) east of Sharjah city*

Encountering desert inhabitants

SHARJAH DESERT PARK
(123 D4) (*K4*)

This desert park was made specially for children and teenagers. In addition to the *Natural History Museum*, the *Botanical Museum* and an aquarium, the *Arabic Wildlife Centre* puts on exhibitions and has desert animals on display. Larger desert animals can be seen in outdoor enclosures from the café, while smaller and nocturnal desert dwellers are kept in the air-conditioned building. The *Children's Farm* is ideal for small children. *Sun / Mon, Wed / Thu 9am–5.30pm, Fri 2pm–5.30pm, Sat 11am–5.30pm | entry 15Dh, free for under 16s | Al-Dhaid Road | Intersection 8 | 25km east of Sharjah (city)*

FESTIVALS & EVENTS

Many holidays and festivals follow the Islamic calendar, based on the lunar calendar. The Islamic year is around 11 days shorter than the Gregorian year. Since the Muslim calendar began on 15 July 622, the year 2012 equates to 1433/34 AH (Anno Hejra). Friday is the weekly day of rest; the 'weekend' is Friday and Saturday.

HOLIDAYS

Hejra (15 Nov 2012, 5 Nov 2013, 25 Oct 2014); **Maulid al-Nabi** Birthday of the Prophet Mohammed (4 Feb 2012, 24 Jan 2013, 13 Jan 2014); **Lailat al-Miraj** Mohammed's ascension to heaven (16 June 2012, 5 June 2013, 25 May 2014); **6 Aug** Accession Day, day when President Sheikh Zayed took office; **2 Dec** National Day, day when the seven emirates became the United Arab Emirates in 1971; **25 Dec** Christmas

MOVEABLE FEASTS

Eid al-Adha is the three-day Festival of Sacrifice at the end of the 10-day period of pilgrimage *(Hadj)* to Mecca. Every Muslim should go on a pilgrimage to Mecca at least once in their life, according to the Koran, as long as their health permits and they are financially able to do so. A sheep is slaughtered and relatives are invited (26–29 Oct 2012, 15–18 Oct 2013, 4–7 Oct 2014). Ramadan is the holy month of Islam, a time of fasting and prayer. From sunrise to sunset Muslims are not allowed to eat, drink or engage in sexual pleasures (20 July–18 Aug 2012, 9 July–7 Aug 2013, 28 June–27 July 2014). Eid al-Fitr is the three-day holiday when the fast is broken at the end of Ramadan with feasts – including in hotels – gift giving and visiting family; people dress up smartly and there are firework displays, fairs and folklore events in the towns and cities (19–21 Aug 2012, 8–10 Aug 2013, 28–30 July 2014).

FESTIVALS & EVENTS

JANUARY/FEBRUARY

The ▶ ● *Dubai Shopping Festival (www.mydsf.com)* attracts visitors with discounts and events from 20 Jan–20 Feb. In mid-January runners meet in Dubai for the ▶ *Dubai Marathon (www.dubaimarathon.org)*.

The world's top golfers show up for four days in mid-January for the

From the horse race with the world's largest prize to the family Water Festival – during the winter there's one event after another

▶ **Abu Dhabi Golf Championship**, held at the 27-hole course of the Abu Dhabi Golf Club *(www.abudhabigolf championship.com)*.

At the ▶ **Sharjah Light Festival** *(www. sharjahlightfestival.ae)*, first held in 2010, 12 striking venues (mosques, squares, souks and museums) are illuminated in many different colours for nine days in mid-February. International light artists create temporary artworks out of light and darkness, colours and patterns.

MARCH

The Arab high society come together for the ▶ **Dubai World Cup**, the horse race with the largest monetary prize in the world *(one week at the end of March, www.dubaiworldcup.com)*.

Since 1993 the Sharjah Art Foundation has been hosting the ▶ **Sharjah Biennale** *(www.sharjahart.org)* for contemporary art in the Sharjah Arts Area. Mid-Mar– mid-May.

SEPTEMBER

During Abu Dhabi's four-day ▶ **International Hunting and Equestrian Exhibition** in mid-September falcons, horses and rifles are the focus of attention *(www. adihex.com)*.

On weekends during the winter season (Oct–Apr) ▶ **camel races** are held on the racecourses of the UAE (Fri and Sat from 7am).

DECEMBER

Folkloristic events, boat races and fire-work displays across the Emirates are held on 2 December to celebrate ▶ **National Day**, when the United Arab Emirates was founded as a state in 1971.

The lively ▶ **Sharjah Water Festival** *(www. swf.ae)* is celebrated for two weeks around Khalid Lagoon with hot-air balloons, firework displays, water-skiing and other shows. The international ▶ **Formula 1 Powerboat World Championship** is held in Sharjah at the same time.

LINKS, BLOGS, APPS & MORE

LINKS

▶ www.marcopolo.de/arabischeemirate Everything at a glance: interactive maps, impression from the community, current news and offers...

▶ www.uaeinteract.com Official website of the UAE with current and tourist news

▶ www.rakpedia.com Private website about Ras al-Khaimah, in-depth and accurate

▶ www.ead.ae The website of the Environment Agency of Abu Dhabi documents the efforts in the nature reserves and protected zones in the Arabian Gulf

▶ www.gulfnews.com Online version of the daily newspaper. Includes news about the UAE, analysis, commentaries and entertainment listings

BLOGS & FORUMS

▶ www.abudhabiwoman.com Expatriate housewives talk about their experiences and the problems of their way of life

▶ fujairahinfocus.blogspot.com Geoff Pond collects insider news and interesting facts from Fujairah. Very comprehensive

▶ dubaithoughts.blogspot.com Life in Dubai – different aspects of living in the city from the perspective of an Australian expatriate

▶ www.secretdubai.blogspot.com 'Secrets', amusing facts, accounts about different aspects of life in the UAE , cynical items, poetry and intrigues, as well as entertaining news, can all be found in this lively blog

VIDEOS

▶ www.dubai-videos.com Lots of videos about attractions, hotels and the architecture of Dubai

▶ www.uaeinteract.com/video Short films about the culture and history of the UAE

Regardless of whether you are still preparing your trip or already in United Arab Emirates: these addresses will provide you with more information, videos and networks to make your holiday even more enjoyable

VIDEOS & STREAMS

▶ www.visitabudhabi.ae/en Has short films about life in Abu Dhabi in its video gallery

▶ mp.marcopolo.de/vae1 Various videos from the United Arab Emirates: trip on Dubai's creek, city architecture, desert, mountains and the sea and a lot more

▶ mp.marcopolo.de/vae2 The web-cam looks at the Yas Marina Formula 1 circuit. Enter 'Dubai' in the search bar to see Burj Al Arab, Jumeirah Beach and Burj Khalifa

APPS

▶ The MARCO POLO CityGuide-App Dubai on your smartphone reliably guides you on your way through the city jungle. Arranged in the useful categories: attractions, food & drink, accommodation, 'in the evening' and others

▶ Various apps about the UAE, such as TravelBook Abu Dhabi with a city map and Dubai Manual with a city map and metro map can be found at www.androidzoom.com/android_applications/uae

▶ The iTunes App Store (www.apple.com/iphone/apps-for-iphone) offers the Dubai City Travel Guide with city maps

▶ The Dubai Department of Tourism (www.dubaitourism.ae) has a free, interactive city map with a search and print function

NETWORKS

▶ www.couchsurfing.org Listed under 'United Arab Emirates', more than 400 native Emiratis and expatriates, men, women and families, offering a couch and sometimes also company to visitors

▶ www.meetup.com will take you to groups with interests and activities between reiki and volleyball if you search under 'Abu Dhabi' and 'Dubai'

▶ socialnetwork.meetup.com Groups look for people to participate in trips, or who are interested in hip hop or entertainment & leisure or who are simply 'newcomers'. Search under 'Abu Dhabi' and 'Dubai'

TRAVEL TIPS

ARRIVAL

There are weekly direct flights to Dubai from the UK; *Emirates (www.emirates.com)* flies every day from London, Newcastle, Manchester, Birmingham, Glasgow, *British Airways (www.britishairways.com)* flies every day from London, as do *Virgin Atlantic (www.virgin-atlantic.com)* and Royal Brunei *(www.bruneiair.com)*. Abu Dhabi's airline *Etihad Airways (www.etihadairways.com)* flies every day from London, Manchester, Chicago, Dallas and New York to Abu Dhabi. *Emirates (www.emirates.com)* flies from Los Angeles, San Francisco, Houston, Toronto and New York to Dubai; flights take between 13 and 16 hours. There are inexpensive flights from London and New York with *Gulf Air (www.gulfair.com)* via Bahrain, and Qatar Airways *(www.qatarairways.com)* via Doha to Dubai. Inexpensive flights between the Gulf states are offered by Fly Dubai *(www.flydubai.com)*, Air Arabia *(www.airarabia.com)*, Jazeera Airways *(www.jazeeraairways)*, Bahrain Air *(www.bahrainair.net)* and RAK Airways *(www.rakairways.com)*.

BANKS & MONEY

You can change money at money exchanges without paying charges or dealing with any other hassle and this is generally an inexpensive way of doing things. You will get a less favourable deal in banks and hotels. Credit cards are widespread. Insert your debit or credit card into an ATM (cash point) and you will be issued with dirhams at that day's rate (plus bank fees). ATMs can be found on every corner and in every shopping mall as well as at the banks.

CARS

The Emirates are connected with each other via motorways; signs are bilingual (Arabic and English). The maximum speed in towns and cities is 50kph (30mph), and 120kph (75mph) outside of urban areas. Roundabouts are more common than intersections (abbreviation: R/A); drivers already on the roundabout have the right of way; more and more flyovers are being built to allow cars to travel without interruption.

CAR HIRE

To hire a car, you'll need a credit card and an international driver's licence; you may also need two passport-sized photos. In some instances rental agencies will hire cars to travellers with only a driver's licence from their own country,

RESPONSIBLE TRAVEL

It doesn't take a lot to be environmentally friendly whilst travelling. Don't just think about your carbon footprint whilst flying to and from your holiday destination but also about how you can protect nature and culture abroad. As a tourist it is especially important to respect nature, look out for local products, cycle instead of driving, save water and much more. If you would like to find out more about eco-tourism please visit: *www.ecotourism.org*

From arrival to weather

From the start to the end of the holiday: useful addresses and information for your trip to United Arab Emirates

but this is happening less often. Prices per day start at about 100Dh, and for four-by-fours from 300Dh. It tends to be cheaper to book from home. You will need an international driver's licence for excursions to Oman.

CLIMATE, WHEN TO GO

The coasts are hot and muggy in the summer (40–45°C/104–113°F); while the interior is dry. Visiting at this time is almost impossible for Europeans. Even the country's inhabitants prefer to stay in air-conditioned rooms during the day in July and August, or they go on holiday to cooler countries. For that reason the main time to go is winter (Oct–Apr), when the climate is mild and the days sunny. Maximum temperatures of 25–35°C (77–95°F), nights 17–20°C (62–68°F).

CONSULATES & EMBASSIES

EMBASSIES OF THE UAE
– 30 Prince's Gate | London SW7 1PT | tel. 0442075811281 | www.uae-embassy.ae/uk
– 3522 International Court, NW | Suite 400 | Washington, DC, 20008 | tel. (202) 243-2400

UK EMBASSY
Khalid bin Al Waleed St (Street 22) | Abu Dhabi | tel. 0971 2 610 1100 | www.ukinuae.fco.gov.uk/en/

US EMBASSY
P.O. Box 4009 | Abu Dhabi, UAE | tel. 0971-2 414 2200 | http://abudhabi.usembassy.gov/index.html

CUSTOMS

200 cigarettes (Abu Dhabi 800) or 100 small cigars or 50 cigars or 250g tobacco and 2l of spirits and 2l of wine can be imported. It is not permitted to bring alcohol into Sharjah. When returning to the EU, you can take 200 cigarettes, 1l spirits and other goods worth up to 2,100Dh.

DESERT TOURS

Stay on the highways through the sand, rubble and marsh deserts. It is better to book a tour through one of the local tour operators.

EMERGENCY

Police tel. 999, fire tel. 997, ambulance tel. 998

HEALTH

There are no required vaccinations, but it is a good idea to have up-to-date vaccinations against tetanus and polio, as well as against hepatitis A. Those who wish to go for a meal outside of the international hotels should be cautious. Although there is no problem with the hygiene, it is best to bring something for digestive problems with you, as you might get struck down by Delhi belly when confronted with unfamiliar foods. Medical care in the UAE is excellent. The doctors are generally English-speaking foreigners. Emergency care is free in the 40 state hospitals and out-patient clinics.

HOTELS

Dubai has best choice of accommodation, with more than 400 hotels, but Abu Dhabi and Sharjah also have a good selection. There are fewer hotels in the four other emirates. In addition to the stated prices, you will have to factor in a 10–15 percent service charge and 10 percent (Dubai) to 15 percent in taxes. It is much cheaper to book hotels through a travel agent or online. The Dubai Tourism website *(www.dubaitourism.ae)* offers a choice of 185 hotels.

HOSTELS

There are well-equipped hostels in Dubai, Sharjah, Fujairah and Khor Fakkan, some of them with double rooms. The hostel in Dubai, for example, is very comfortable and also suitable for families; it has a cafeteria, tennis, pool and a bus stop (No. 34) just outside. You don't need to be a member of Hostelling International. *Information: UAE Youth Hostels Association | P.O. Box 94141 | Al-Qusais Road 39 | Dubai | tel. 04 2 98 81 61 | www.uaeyha. com. Open: Dubai 24 hrs, otherwise: check-in 9am–1pm and 5pm–8pm, closed after midnight.*

BUDGETING

Taxi	0.50–0.75 £ / 0.85–1.25 $	per km incl. basic charge
Mocha	2.50 £ / 4 $	per cup
Lounger	5–6 £ / 8–9 $	per day for two
Wine	from 12 £ / 20 $	for a bottle in a restaurant
Petrol	approx. 0.25 £ / 0.40 $	for 1 l premium
Kebab	3–4 £ / 4–5 $	for one skewer and flat bread

IMMIGRATION & ONWARD TRAVEL

On arrival at an airport in the UAE, travellers will be issued with a 'visa on arrival' (valid for 30 days) free of charge. This visa is stamped into the passport; make sure your passport is valid for six months from the date of your arrival.

With a visa from either the UAE or Oman travellers can get a visa for the other country at the (land) border crossings. When driving from Al Ain (Abu Dhabi) to Muscat (Oman), you will have to pay a *UAE-vehicle fee* (20Dh) as well as 20 OR/200Dh for an Omani visa. The visa fee for trips from Ras al-Khaimah (UAE) to Khasab (Oman) is 20 OR (200Dh); on your return you will have to pay 2 OR (20Dh) for the Omani vehicle fee. From the emirate of Dubai via Hatta to Oman and vice versa: no visa fee, but a 2 OR (20Dh) *vehicle fee*. When driving across the border between UAE and Oman you have to pay a car insurance fee (approx. 8–10 OR/80–100Dh per day), so take this into account when hiring a car. Those entering Oman from Ras al-Khaimah near Tibat (towards Khasab) will have to leave by the same way.

INFORMATION

ABU DHABI TOURISM AUTHORITY
– No1. Knightsbridge | London SW1X 7LY | tel. 0207 201 6400 | www.visitabu habi.ae | www.abudhabitourism.ae | www.exploreabudhabi.ae
– 1120 Avenue of the Americas, Suite 4047 | New York, NY 10036 | tel. 01 212 338 0101 | www.visitabu dhabi.ae | www.abudhabitourism.ae | www.exploreabudhabi.ae

DUBAI DEPARTMENT OF TOURISM
– 4th floor Nuffield House | 41–46 Piccadilly | London, W1J 0DS | tel. 020 7321

*6110 | www.dubaitourism.ae | dtcm_uk@ dubaitourism.ae
– 25 West 45th Street, Suite #405 | New York, NY 10036 | 001 212 575 2262 | www.dubaitourism.ae | dtcm_usa@dubaitourism.ae*

FUJAIRAH TOURISM BUREAU

Trade Centre | Hamad Bin Abdullah Road | Fujairah, UAE | tel. 009719 2 231554 | www.fujairah-tourism.gov.ae

RAS AL-KHAIMAH TOURISM OFFICE

P.O. Box 31291 | Al-Jazirat Al-Hamra | Ras al-Khaimah | tel. 009717 2 44 5125 | www.raktourism.com

SHARJAH TOURISM AUTHORITY

Crescent Tower, 9th Floor | PO Box: 26661 | Sharjah, UAE | tel. 097165566777 | www.sharjahtourism.ae
To find out about current events, consult TimeOut Dubai *(weekly, 7Dh, www.timeoutdubai.com);* TimeOut Abu Dhabi *(weekly, 7Dh)* as well as the informative What's On *(monthly 10Dh)* for both cities.

INTERNET ACCESS & WIFI

Almost all the hotels in the UAE have internet facilities for guests, often free. WiFi is not yet very widespread. Hotspots can also be found at *www.hotspotlocations.com.*

PHONE & MOBILE PHONE

The international dialling code of the UAE is 00971. To call the UK from the UAE, dial 0044; to call the US, dial 001. Making a telephone call is easy and inexpensive in a telephone booth with a telephone card (30, 50, 100Dh).
Mobile phones are called GSM or *cell phones in the UAE.* The network operator is the telephone company *Etisalat (tel. 101 | www.etisalat.co.ae).* If you have a prepaid card for the UAE, there are no fees for incoming calls. Your voice mail will incur high fees, so it's best to switch it off before you arrive.
Visitors can buy a local mobile phone number *(visitor mobile line)* from Etisalat in duty-free shops, at the airport and in Etisalat branches: *cost 80Dh with 20Dh in credit, valid for 90 days.* Of interest to tourists, Etisalat branches and supermarkets (such as Carrefour) sell local prepaid SIM cards for 75Dh with 25Dh in credit; you will need your passport to buy one.

PHOTOGRAPHY

Only take pictures of individual people after obtaining their permission. For religious

CURRENCY CONVERTER

£	Dh	Dh	£
1	5.80	1	0.17
3	17.40	3	0.51
5	29	5	0.86
13	75.40	13	2.24
40	232	40	6.90
75	435	75	12.90
120	696	120	20.70
250	1,450	250	43
500	2,900	500	86

$	Dh	Dh	$
1	3.70	1	0.27
3	11	3	0.82
5	18.30	5	1.36
13	47.75	13	3.54
40	147	40	10.90
75	275	75	20
120	440	120	33
250	918	250	68
500	1,836	500	136

For current exchange rates see www.xe.com

reasons it is not acceptable to take pictures of Muslim women, unless they expressly agree to it. You also must not take pictures of military facilities, police stations and port facilities or airports. Ask the guards before taking pictures of the rulers' palaces.

POST

Post offices can be found in all larger towns and neighbourhoods. A postcard to Europe costs 3Dh.

PRICES & CURRENCY

The currency in the UAE is the dirham (Dh, AED), and 1 dirham breaks down into 100 fils. The UAE is not a cheap destination, and hotels in Dubai and Abu Dhabi are particularly expensive. Nevertheless there are significant differences in prices depending on whether you choose to eat in your hotel restaurant or in the Indian place around the corner. In the first case it costs more than at home; in the second case a lot less.

PUBLIC TRANSPORT

Although there are city buses in Abu Dhabi, Al Ain and Sharjah, their destinations are either stated in Arabic script only or

WEATHER IN DUBAI

	Jan	Feb	March	April	May	June	July	Aug	Sept	Oct	Nov	Dec
Daytime temperatures in °C/°F												
	20/68	21/70	24/75	28/82	33/91	35/95	37/99	38/100	36/97	32/90	27/81	22/72
Nighttime temperatures in °C/°F												
	14/57	15/59	17/63	21/70	26/79	28/82	29/84	30/86	27/81	24/75	21/70	16/61
Sunshine hours/day												
	8/46	8/46	8/46	10/50	12/54	12/54	10/50	10/50	10/50	10/50	9/48	8/46
Precipitation days/month												
	1	2	1	2	0	0	0	0	0	0	1	1
Water temperature in °C/°F												
	19/66	18/64	23/73	27/81	27/81	27/81	29/84	32/90	27/81	27/81	25/77	24/75

not at all, so they are used almost exclusively by Asian migrant workers. There are not many buses in the other emirates. Locals take their cars, and tourists tend to take taxis. One good option is to hire a car at the airport in Abu Dhabi, because it's relatively easy to find your way around there and the journeys within the emirate (such as to the south and to Liwa Oasis) are quite long.

In Dubai, tourists can conveniently get to most attractions by metro, which is an aerial railway across large sections of the city, with great views. There are also several city buses whose destinations are indicated in English too (*Daypass Metro, Bus, Waterbus 16Dh*).

Regular buses (Emirates Express) run between Dubai and Abu Dhabi, Al-Ain, Hatta, Fujairah, *6am–10pm, ticket price 15–25Dh*.

TAXI

A taxi in Dubai costs 3.50Dh as the basic fee (20Dh from the airport and to Sharjah) and 1.70Dh/km. It is a little bit more at night and on public holidays. In Abu Dhabi and Sharjah taxis also have a taximeter and the prices are even lower. Dubai has women's taxis, which can be recognized by their pink roof and pink interiors (as well as a woman driver, of course). A trip from Dubai to Abu Dhabi or Fujairah costs around 250Dh, or 450Dh there and back. In the other emirates the taxi fare has to be negotiated.

TIPPING

A 10 percent tip is only expected in restaurants when the *service charge* is not already included in the bill; but that is rarely the case. Baggage porters get 3Dh per item, while it's customary to round up the fare in a taxi. Room attendants get 5Dh per day.

TIME

GMT plus 4 hours, during the summer time plus 3 hours.

SPELLING

The transliteration of Arabic into the Latin alphabet is done by ear and everyone hears something slightly different: jebel, djebel, jabal, jebal. MARCO POLO uses the spelling also used by the locals, which tends to be the English-language option, as this is usually used on bilingual signs.

SWIMMING

It is better to visit the beach clubs since public beaches (open beaches) do not have any facilities and Western tourists will also have to contend with gawping expatriates from Asia. Swimming is a problem on some beaches because of strong undercurrents. Lifeguards and warning red flags are found only at the hotels' private beaches and in the beach parks, which have an entry fee. *Beach parks include Dubai: Jumeirah Beach Park (700m/765 yard beach) | Sun–Wed 8am–10pm, Thu–Sat 8am–11pm | Mon women and children only | Jumeirah Road | entry 5Dh. Abu Dhabi:Corniche Beach | daily 7am–11pm | entry 5Dh | Corniche Road West.*

WHAT TO WEAR

The climate is very mild in winter, so summer clothes will suffice all year round. But bring a pullover for the hotel rooms, restaurants and shopping malls, as the air-conditioning can feel chilly: it will also be useful for the occasional cool winter night. Clothing etiquette in the region frowns on shorts, bare shoulders and, for women, anything that is tight, short or transparent.

NOTES

MARCO POLO TRAVEL GUIDES

ALGARVE
AMSTERDAM
AUSTRALIA
BANGKOK
BARCELONA
BERLIN
BRUSSELS
BUDAPEST
CALIFORNIA
CAPE TOWN
  WINE LANDS,
  GARDEN ROUTE
COLOGNE
CORFU
GRAN CANARIA
CRETE
CUBA
CYPRUS
  NORTH AND SOUTH
DUBAI

DUBROVNIK &
  DALMATIAN COAST
EDINBURGH
EGYPT
FINLAND
FLORENCE
FLORIDA
FRENCH RIVIERA
  NICE, CANNES &
  MONACO
HONGKONG
  MACAU
IRELAND
ISRAEL
ISTANBUL
JORDAN
KOS

LAKE GARDA
LANZAROTE
LAS VEGAS
LONDON
LOS ANGELES
MADEIRA
  PORTO SANTO
MALLORCA
MALTA
  GOZO
MOROCCO
NEW YORK
NEW ZEALAND
NORWAY
PARIS
RHODES

ROME
SAN FRANCISCO
SICILY
SOUTH AFRICA
STOCKHOLM
TENERIFE
THAILAND
TURKEY
  SOUTH COAST
UNITED ARAB
  EMIRATES
VENICE
VIETNAM

- PACKED WITH INSIDER TIPS
- BEST WALKS AND TOURS
- FULL-COLOUR PULL-OUT MAP
  AND STREET ATLAS

ROAD ATLAS

The green line ▬▬ indicates the Trips & Tours (p. 94–99)
The blue line ▬▬ indicates The perfect route (p. 30–31)

All tours are also marked on the pull-out map

Photo: Dubai Creek with abra

Exploring the United Arab Emirates

The map on the back cover shows how the area has been sub-divided

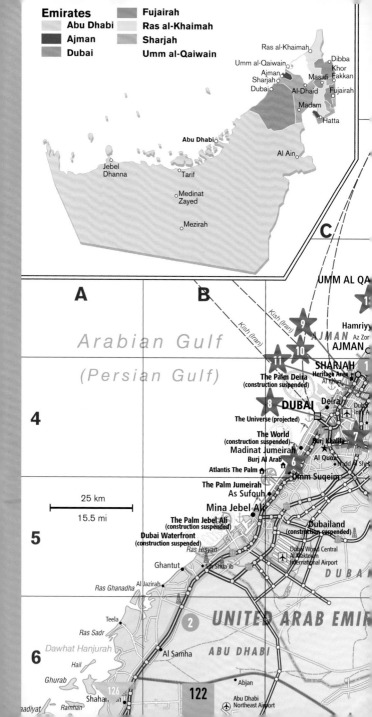

Emirates

- **Abu Dhabi**
- **Ajman**
- **Dubai**
- Fujairah
- Ras al-Khaimah
- Sharjah
- Umm al-Qaiwain

Ras al-Khaimah

Umm al-Qaiwain
Ajman
Sharjah
Dubai

Dibba
Khor
Fakkan
Masafi
Al-Dhaid
Fujairah
Madam
Hatta

Abu Dhabi

Al Ain

Jebel
Dhanna

Tarif

Medinat
Zayed

Mezirah

C

A

B

UMM AL QA

Arabian Gulf

(Persian Gulf)

Kish (Iran)

Kish (Iran)

9

10

11

Hamriyy

AJMAN   Az Zor

AJMAN

SHARJAH
Heritage Area
Al Khan

The Palm Deira
(construction suspended)

8 **DUBAI**

Deira

Dub
Int'l A

The Universe (projected)

The World
(construction suspended)
Madinat Jumeirah

Burj Al Arab

Atlantis The Palm

The Palm Jumeirah
As Sufouh

Mina Jebel Ali

The Palm Jebel Ali
(construction suspended)

Dubai Waterfront
(construction suspended)

Ghantut

Ras Hisyan

Ras Shua'ib

Al Jazirah

Ras Ghanadha

Teela

Ras Sadr

Dawhat Hanjurah

Hail

Ghurab

aadiyat   Ramhan

Shaha...

Burj Khalifa

Al Quoz

Nadd Al She

Umm Suqeim

7

6

4

5

6

25 km

15.5 mi

Dubailand
(construction suspended)

Dubai World Central
Al Maktoum
International Airport

2 **UNITED ARAB EMIR**

DUBA

ABU DHABI

Al Samha

Abjan

126

122

Abu Dhabi
Northeast Airport

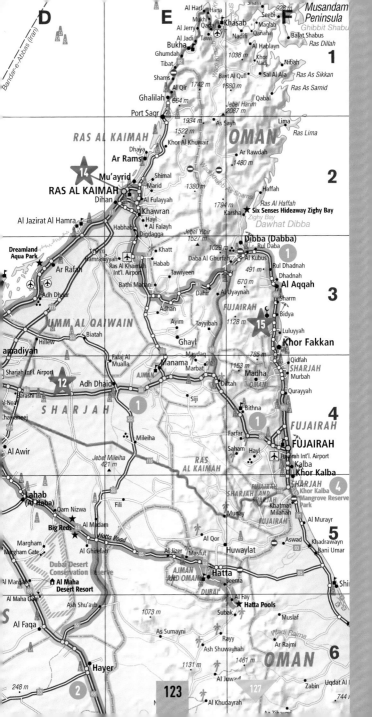

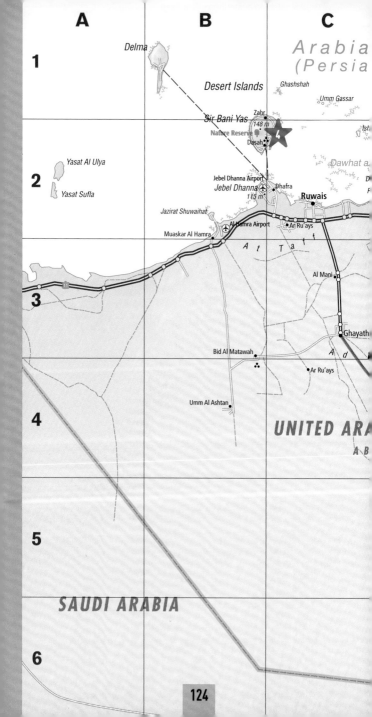

1

Delma

Desert Islands   Ghashshah

Arabia
(Persia

Umm Gassar

Ish

Sir Bani Yas   Zabr
148 m

Nature Reserve   ★4

Dasah

Dawhat a.

2

Yasat Al Ulya

Yasat Sufla

Jebel Dhanna Airport ✈
Jebel Dhanna ✈   Dhafra
115 m

D

Ruwais   P

Jazirat Shuwaihat

Al Hamra Airport ✈
Muaskar Al Hamra   Ar Ru'ays

A t   T   a   f

3

Al Mani

Ghayath

Bid Al Matawah

A   d

• Ar Ru'ays

Umm Al Ashtan

4

UNITED ARA

A   B

5

SAUDI ARABIA

6

124

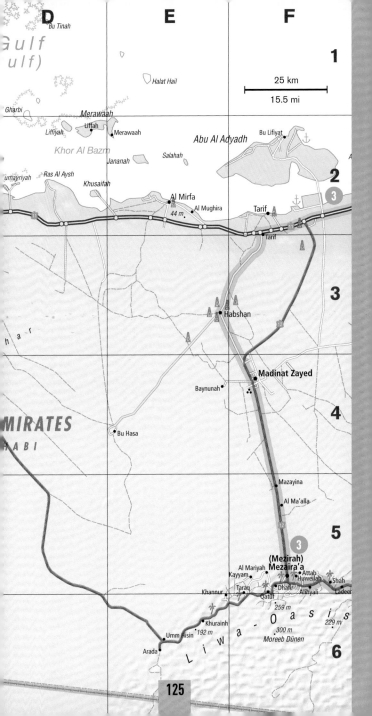

D
E
F

1

Bu Tinah

Gulf
ulf)

Halat Hail

25 km
15.5 mi

Gharbi

Merawaah

Liffah

Liffiyah

Merawaah

Abu Al Adyadh

Bu Lifiyat

Khor Al Bazm

Jananah

Salahah

umayriyah

Ras Al Aysh

Khusaifah

2

Al Mirfa
44 m.

Al Mughira

Tarif

Tarif

3

h a r

Habshan

3

Madinat Zayed

Baynunah

4

MIRATES

H A B I

Bu Hasa

Mazayina

Al Ma'alla

5

3

(Mezirah)
Mezaira'a

Al Mariyah

Kayyam

Attab

Huweilah

Shah

Khannur

Taraq

Dhafir

Alihyali

Ladeer

Qatuf
259 m

O a s i s

229 m

Khurainh
192 m

Umm Hisin

L i w a

300 m
Moreeb Dünen

6

Arada

125

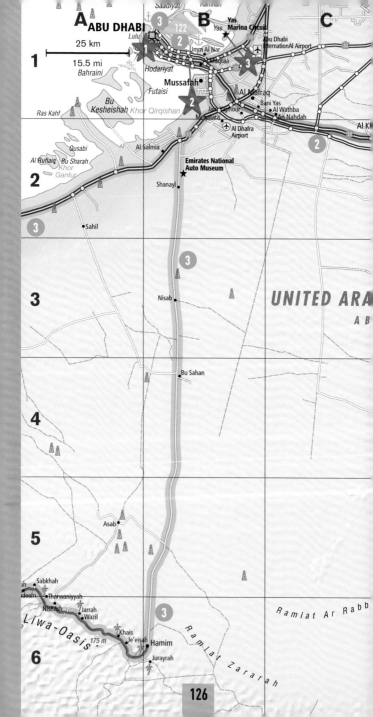

A   ABU DHABI   B   C

25 km
15.5 mi

Saadiyat
Yas
Yas Marina Circuit
Lulu
Abu Dhabi
InternationAl Airport
Umm Al Nar
Bahraini
Maqtaa
Hodariyat
Futaisi
Mussafah
Bu Kesheishah   Khor Qirqishan
Al Mafraq
Ras Kahf
Jabel Dhanour
Bani Yas
Al Wathba
Mussafah
An Nahdah
Al Dhafra Airport
Al KI
Qusabi
Bu Sharah
Al Salmia
Al Ruflaiq
Khor Gantur
Emirates National
Auto Museum
Shanayl

Sahil

Nisab

UNITED ARA
A B

Bu Sahan

Asab

Sabkhah
Tharwaniyyah
Nishash   Jarrah
Liwa-Oasis   Wazil
175 m
Khais   Je'eisah   Hamim
Jurayrah

Ramlat Ar Rabb

Ramlat Zararah

126

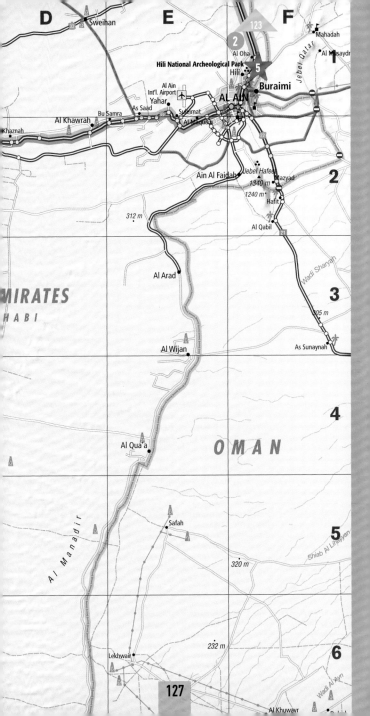

D

Sweihan

E

F

Mahadah

Jebel Qatar

Al Musaydir

1

123

2

Al Oha

5

Hili National Archeological Park

Hili

Buraimi

Yahar

Al Ain
Int'l. Airport

AL AIN

As Saad

Sulaimat

Bu Samra

Al Khawrah

Al Maqqab

Khaznah

22

Ain Al Faidah

Jebel Hafeet
1340 m
1240 m*

Mazyad

2

Hafit

312 m

Al Qabil

21

Wadi Sharyah

EMIRATES

HABI

Al Arad

3

305 m

As Sunaynah

Al Wijan

O M A N

4

Al Qua'a

Al Manadir

Safah

5

320 m

Shiab Al Lihayyan

232 m

6

Lekhwair

127

Wadi Al Ayn

Al Khuwayr

KEY TO ROAD ATLAS

Motorway with junction / Autobahn mit Anschlussstelle
Dual carriage-way with junction / Schnellstraße mit Anschlussstelle
Highway / Fernstraße
Main road / Hauptstraße
Other road / Nebenstraße
Non-asphalted road / Straße, nicht befestigt
Carrige way / Fahrweg
Dirt track / Piste
Road under construction; scheduled / Straße in Bau; geplant
Closed road / Straße für Kfz gesperrt
Tunnel
Railway / Eisenbahn
Ferry, shipping route / Fähre, Schiffsverbindung
Channel / Kanal
National border / Staatsgrenze
Emirate border / Provinzgrenze
Pipeline
National park; nature reserve / Nationalpark; Naturpark
Prohibited area / Sperrgebiet
Harbour / Hafen
International airport / Internationaler Flughafen
National airport, airfield / Nationaler Flughafen; Flugplatz
Fort, castle; ruin / Fort, Festung; Ruine
Sightseeing; Museum / Sehenswürdigkeit; Museum
Mosque, archeological site / Moschee; Archäologische Stätte
Tower; lighthouse / Turm; Leuchtturm
Waterfall; cave / Wasserfall; Höhle
Mountain top; pass / Berggipfel; Pass, Joch
Beach; hot spring / Badestrand; Heiße Quelle
Border crossing / Grenzübergang
Oasis; sea-angling / Oase; Hochseefischen
Information; theatre / Information; Theater
Golf course; zoo / Golfplatz; Zoo
Camping; viewpoint / Campingplatz; Aussichtspunkt
Hotel, resort; hospital / Hotel, Resort; Krankenhaus
Police; post / Polizei; Post
Busstation; monument / Busbahnhof; Denkmal, Monument
Trips & Tours / Ausflüge & Touren
Perfect route / Perfekte Route

 MARCO POLO Highlights

INDEX

This index lists all places and sites featured in this guide. Numbers in bold indicate a main entry.

DOS & DON'TS

In the Emirates too there are some things that are best avoided

FAMILY HOLIDAYS IN THE SUMMERTIME

Temperatures rise to way over 40°C (104°F) during summer and you'll even burn your feet on the sand on your way to the water. That makes spending time in the Emirates an unpleasant affair for children. If you would like to take advantage of the high discounts that the hotels offer during the summer, you should definitely leave the children at home.

SHOWING YOUR MIDRIFF IN SHARJAH

According to the regulations, it is not permitted in the Emirate of Sharjah to walk around in beachwear (meaning in a bikini top or in a swimsuit with a skirt) or in any other 'offensive' manner in the city; you could face a fine or even arrest.

ATTRACTING ATTENTION WITH TOO MUCH ALCOHOL

Some restaurants and hotels in the Emirates will serve you any drink you could ask for. And it's fine to enjoy them. But anyone who attracts attention for being inebriated will have problems that could even include prison.

LOOKING FOR YOUR OWN TABLE IN A RESTAURANT

Even in the small, basic Asian restaurants it is not done for guests to look for their own table. Wait to be seated (it's okay to ask for a specific table). That goes down well because it's what everyone does.

FORGETTING YOUR PASSPORT ON A NIGHT OUT

Bars and nightclubs are only open to people above the age of 21. Some night lubs inspect every guest's passport.

GOING TO THE DESERT ALONE

Those travelling in a rental car without four-wheel drive should not leave the road and drive into the desert. Although the sand is flat and seems firm, tourists will not spot the soft 'holes'. Suddenly you will become stuck, unable to move your car.

TRAVELLING DURING RAMADAN

Public life is severely limited during the annual month of fasting. Shops and restaurants only open after sunset, the hotel lobbies are deserted and taxis are hard to come by. Often food and drink are only available after dark, or from room service.

WADI BASHING

Trips into the desert and the wadis in a four-by-four destroy the desert plants that struggle to grow in the poor desert soil – this is entertainment at the expense of the environment.

CREDITS

WRITE TO US

e-mail: info@marcopologuides.co.uk

Did you have a great holiday?
Is there something on your mind?
Whatever it is, let us know!
Whether you want to praise, alert us to errors or give us a personal tip – MARCO POLO would be pleased to hear from you.
We do everything we can to provide the very latest information for your trip.

Nevertheless, despite all of our authors' thorough research, errors can creep in. MARCO POLO does not accept any liability for this. Please contact us by e-mail or post.

MARCO POLO Travel Publishing Ltd
Pinewood, Chineham Business Park
Crockford Lane, Chineham
Basingstoke, Hampshire RG24 8AL
United Kingdom

PICTURE CREDITS

Cover photograph: camel herd, Look: age fotostock
Images: G. Amberg (28/29, 74); Arabian Ranches Golf Club: Mike Klemme (16 top); DuMont Bildarchiv: Heimbach (3 bottom, 86/87); Fasateen-Zareeana (16 centre); © fotolia.com: Suresh Thiagarajan (16 bottom); R. Freyer (2 centre top, 2 bottom, 3 top, 32/33, 45, 52, 60/61, 65, 72/73, 80, 88, 112 bottom); R. centre Gill (3 centre, 5, 6, 8, 26 l., 26 r., 30 l., 30 r., 47, 78/79, 82/83, 93, 97, 104/105, 107, 112 top); R. Hackenberg (13, 91); Huber: Borchi (106), Gräfenhain (113), Pavan (62), Schmid (10/11, 18/19, 28, 40, 42/43, 68, 94/95, 124/125); © iStockphoto.com: Madeleine Openshaw (17 bottom); centre Kirchgessner (2 top, 4, 23, 24/25, 36, 58/59, 108/109, 109); Laif: Krause (27, 100/101, 108), Martin (20), Sasse (29, 54); Laif/REA/Financial Times: Bibby (38); Look: age fotostock (flap r., 1 top, 71); mauritius images: Alamy (7, 56); mauritius images/imagebroker: Gerhard (49), Lippert (2 centre bottom, 50/51), Tack (9, 34, 98/99); D. Renckhoff (flap l., 15, 67, 76, 84, 92, 102); Charlene Rennit: Kwame Busia (17 top); centre Wöbcke (1 bottom)

1st Edition 2013

Worldwide Distribution: Marco Polo Travel Publishing Ltd, Pinewood, Chineham Business Park, Crockford Lane, Basingstoke, Hampshire RG24 8AL, United Kingdom. Email: sales@marcopolouk.com
© MAIRDUMONT GmbH & Co. KG, Ostfildern
Chief editors: Michaela Lienemann (concept, managing editor), Marion Zorn (concept, text editor)
Author: Manfred Wöbcke; editor: Petra Klose
Programme supervision: Anita Dahlinger, Ann-Katrin Kutzner, Nikolai Michaelis
Picture editor: Gabriele Forst
What's hot: wunder media, Munich;
Cartography road atlas: DuMont Reisekartografie, Fürstenfeldbruck; © MAIRDUMONT, Ostfildern;
Cartography pull-out map: DuMont Reisekartografie, Fürstenfeldbruck; © MAIRDUMONT, Ostfildern
Design: milchhof : atelier, Berlin; Front cover, pull-out map cover, page 1: factor product munich
Translated from German by Michael Scuffil, Leverkusen; editor of the English edition: Dorothy Stannard, London
Prepress: BW-Medien GmbH, Leonberg